101 THINGS EVERYONE SHOULD KNOW ABOUT
JUDAISM

Beliefs, Practices, Customs, and Traditions

Richard D. Bank

James B. Wiggins, Ph.D., *Series Editor*

ADAMS MEDIA
AVON, MASSACHUSETTS

Published by Adams Media,
an F+W Publications Company
57 Littlefield Street
Avon, MA 02322
www.adamsmedia.com
ISBN 13: 978-1-59337-327-6
ISBN 10: 1-59337-327-9

Printed in Canada.

J I H G F E D C B
Library of Congress Cataloging-in-Publication Data
Bank, Richard D.
101 things everyone should know about Judaism / Richard D. Bank ; edited by James B. Wiggins.
p.   cm.
ISBN 1-59337-327-9
1. Judaism—Doctrines. 2. Judaism—Customs and practices.
I. Title: One hundred one things everyone should know about Judaism. II. Title: One hundred
and one things everyone should know about Judaism. III. Wiggins, James B. IV. Title.

BM602.B36 2005
296—dc22

2005007440

This publication is designed to provide accurate and authoritative information with regard to the
subject matter covered. It is sold with the understanding that the publisher is not engaged in ren-
dering legal, accounting, or other professional advice. If legal advice or other expert assistance is
required, the services of a competent professional person should be sought.
—From a *Declaration of Principles* jointly adopted by a Committee of the American Bar Association
and a Committee of Publishers and Associations

Interior illustration © Brand X Pictures
This book is available at quantity discounts for bulk purchases.
For information, please call 1-800-289-0963.

Contents

Introduction ix

  1. What does being Jewish mean? 1

PART 1: THE DEVELOPMENT OF JUDAISM 3

  2. Joseph's saga and the journey to Egypt:
      The historical context of Passover 5

  3. The Exodus: Deliverance from slavery in Egypt 7

  4. Schism and rebellion: The historical context of Hanukkah 10

  5. The Maccabean Rebellion and the reclaiming of the Temple 12

  6. Exile in Persia: The historical context of Purim 13

  7. Esther makes her case and the Jews prevail 16

  8. Branches of Judaism under Greek and Roman rule 17

  9. The difference between Karaitic,
      Ashkenazic, and Sephardic Jews 20

10. Orthodox Judaism 22

11. Reform Judaism 25

12. Conservative Judaism 27

13. The emergence of Reconstructionism
     in twentieth-century America 29

14. The schism between mystics and traditionalists,
     and the beginning of Hasidism 32

15. Hasidic practices today 35

PART 2: ESSENTIAL BELIEFS AND LAWS 37

16. The Torah: Judaism's cornerstone......................... 39

17. The Talmud: Applying the laws of the Bible to life............ 41

18. Using the responsa tradition
       to answer contemporary questions 44

19. Midrashim: Interpretive stories 45

20. Halakah: Jewish law and accumulated jurisprudence.......... 47

21. The Ten Statements 49

22. The 613 mitzvot...................................... 51

23. Other laws: Geizeirah, takkanah, minhag, and lashon ha-ra..... 54

24. Basic tenets: The Thirteen Principles of Faith................ 56

25. Striving to comprehend the nature of God................... 59

26. The eternal nature of the soul............................ 62

27. The Jewish concept of the afterlife 63

28. Resurrection and the world to come....................... 65

29. Honoring the dead.................................... 67

30. Spirituality and mysticism: Connecting to divine sparks........ 70

31. The Kabbalah.. 72

32. Understanding God's essence
       through the Kabbalistic Tree of Life 75

33. Establishing justice through good deeds 76

34. The Jewish outlook on interfaith marriage and divorce 78

35. What does keeping kosher mean?......................... 80

PART 3: RELIGIOUS SERVICES AND OBJECTS **83**

36. What it means to be a rabbi 85

37. What does a cantor do? 87

38. The importance of prayer 89

39. House of prayer: The synagogue 91

40. Prayer during formal worship 93

41. Blessings 96

42. Important things to know
   when attending a Jewish service 98

43. Items found in the synagogue 100

44. "Laying" tefillin 102

45. Why do Jews wear skullcaps, prayer shawls, and tassels? 103

46. Judaic decorations: The Star of David,
   the chai, and the hamesh 105

47. The mezuzah and other religious items
   found in Jewish homes 106

PART 4: HOLY DAYS AND FESTIVALS **109**

48. Observing Shabbat 111

49. Why are certain activities prohibited during Shabbat? 113

50. Shabbat services 115

51. What do Jewish families do during Shabbat? 116

52. Seeking forgiveness and reconciliation
   during the Days of Awe 120

53. Rosh Hashanah: The Jewish New Year 122

54. Rosh Hashanah ceremonies, customs, and services 124

55. Yom Kippur: The Day of Atonement 126

56. Which activities are prohibited on Yom Kippur? 128

57. Yom Kippur preparations and services 129

58. The significance of Sukkot 132

59. Building and using a sukkah 134

60. Sukkot services and liturgy 137

61. Shemini Atzeret: The Assembly of the Eighth Day. 139

62. Simchat Torah: Completing the cycle of readings 140

63. Hanukkah's religious significance 143

64. Lighting the Hanukkah menorah 146

65. Hanukkah customs, traditions, and services 147

66. Purim observances and celebrations. 149

67. A time for rejoicing and celebrating 152

68. Recognizing the hidden face of God
    and the power of the individual. 154

69. What is chametz?. 155

70. Passover services and observances. 156

71. The Passover seder 159

72. Key elements of the seder ceremony 162

73. Shavuot: The Festival of Weeks 164

74. Shavuot services 167

75. Tisha B'Av: Memorializing the destruction of the Temples 168

76. Tu B'Shevat: New Year for Trees 171

PART 5: CEREMONIES AND MILESTONES 173

77. Finding a soul mate through a matchmaker................. 175

78. The Jewish view of marriage............................. 176

79. Mitzvot that deal with marriage and sexual relations.......... 178

80. Kiddushin and the ketubah:
    Betrothal and marriage contract 181

81. Key elements in a Jewish wedding ceremony 183

82. Marking the birth of a new child........................ 187

83. The Jewish view on adoption and abortion................. 188

84. The importance of naming ceremonies
    and the circumcision ritual 190

85. Redemption ceremonies............................... 194

86. Bar and bat mitzvah: Becoming sons and daughters
    of the commandment 196

87. The bar and bat mitzvah ceremonies 199

88. Parties, feasts, and other activities to
    celebrate bar and bat mitzvahs 201

89. Confirmation: Celebrating continued education 204

90. Jewish funeral ceremonies 205

91. What does sitting shiva mean?.......................... 207

92. The final phases of mourning........................... 210

PART 6: JEWISH CUSTOM, CULTURE, AND TRADITION 213

93. The Hebrew language as a common thread 215

94. The sacred language and the mother tongue 219

95. Hebrew's renaissance in the nineteenth
    and twentieth centuries.............................. 222

96. The history of Yiddish literature........................ 224

97. The rise of modern Jewish writing 226

98. Yiddish poetry, drama, journalism, and music
    in the twentieth century and beyond 227

99. Jewish cuisine....................................... 229

100. Common food dishes................................. 231

101. Jewish humor as a means of speaking
     about existential questions.......................... 235

APPENDIX: TIMELINE OF KEY EVENTS: HINDUISM, JUDAISM,
    CHRISTIANITY, BUDDHISM, AND ISLAM 239

Unlike many other religious traditions, Judaism does not trace its origins to the life and teachings of a single individual. Rather it is like a cable or rope that gathers its strength by intertwining multiple strands of diverse events and memories, stories, significant people, writings produced through the centuries, rituals, and holiday traditions.

Although Jews have never been a group large in number (there are 13 to 14 million Jews worldwide, and they comprise just .02 percent of the world's population), the influence of their ideals, aspirations, and actions has been far greater than their size might imply. Judaism's central affirmation of one God who is the creator and sustainer of the world and all humanity is one of the earliest expressions of monotheism. Further, Jews have widely accepted the belief that knowledge of God (Yahweh) and His will for human morality and ethics has come to Judaism through revelation. Over centuries Judaism has created a canon of sacred writings to encapsulate this revelation, beginning with the Torah, prophetic views, and wisdom writings (notably the Psalms and Proverbs), which were collected into what is now known as the Hebrew Bible.

The Torah—the first five books of the Hebrew Bible, in which Moses' integral role figures prominently—is revered by all of the diverse communities that have been a part of Judaism through the ages. However, having lived in many different cultural and political settings for more more than twenty-five centuries, Jews have repeatedly had to reinterpret and adapt their worldviews and lifestyles to changing situations. And so, alongside the writings, Judaism's tradition developed further into what is called the *Mishnah*, or Oral Torah, and the *Talmud*, rabbinical interpretations of the Torah. These works were also collected in written form in the first centuries of the Common Era.

Different branches of Judaism—including Orthodox, Reform, Conservative, and Reconstructionist—have developed over time, and each branch interprets scripture and oral teachings in its own distinctive way. And yet one touchstone stands out in all of Judaism's various forms: the theme of exile and restoration (or return). The Hebrews' enslavement in Egypt and their escape into the Sinai Desert, led by Moses and his brother Aaron, exemplify the stories so often retold in Jewish history. Once again, during biblical times, the Hebrews' imprisonment in Babylonia in the sixth century B.C.E. was followed by a return to Israel when the Persians liberated them.

This cycle of exile and return continued into the Common Era, through the Middle Ages and beyond. For example, from the seventh through the thirteenth centuries, during the time of Islamic rule over much of modern-day Spain, the Jews flourished. Then, during the fifteenth century the Jews were expelled from this region and were not allowed to return to Europe until centuries later. This theme continued to play out, right into more recent times when, in the nineteenth century, the Jews' desire to return to Palestine and have a home of their own developed into the idea and ideal of Zionism. After Nazi Germany perpetrated the almost unimaginable decimation of European Jews during the Holocaust in the twentieth century, the Jews' dream of having a home of their own was finally realized when the state of Israel was created in 1948.

Today, Jews from anywhere and everywhere in the world can now claim citizenship there.

Indeed, there is much to relay about the Jewish saga, not only in terms of religious faith, but history and culture as well. Yet Judaism's legacy also reaches beyond its own heritage and tradition; its profound influence extends to both Christianity and Islam, which are daughters of Judaism. Although much larger than their mother in numerical terms, both traditions, along with Judaism, hold fast to the reality of one God, assert the centrality of ethical norms and moral behavior, and perpetuate a hope for the fulfillment of the promises their traditions carry.

Within the pages of this book, you'll glean an understanding of Judaism's complex history and learn about some of the many forms of Judaism that have emerged over the centuries. You'll also become familiar with key Jewish holidays, rituals, beliefs, services, celebrations, and many other practices, which will, no doubt, leave you with a deeper awareness of and appreciation for this rich tradition.

Some people have concluded that there is no greater proof of the existence of God than the survival of the Jews amid all they have endured throughout their tumultuous history. Keep reading and decide for yourself.

— 1 —

WHAT DOES BEING JEWISH MEAN?

Judaism is a tradition with a long history. In spite of many changes, trials, and tribulations, it has endured for thousands of years, demonstrating an amazing ability to survive while remaining true to its essence. Judaism developed the concept of monotheism, the belief in one God, and served as the foundation for Christianity and Islam. All of these accomplishments, and more, make Judaism a religion worthy of study.

The word *Judaism* does not appear anywhere in the Bible or in early rabbinical literature. Hellenized Jews actually introduced this concept in the second century B.C.E. to describe their religious practice.

Judaism is more than just a religion, however—it is also a way of life. Through the ages, Jews have been regarded as a "people," a "nation" (though, for most of its existence, one without a homeland), a "race," and a "culture." Because it is such a comprehensive term, it is difficult to pinpoint all of the many facets that encompass and define Judaism.

Over the course of history, non-Jews often took it upon themselves to define what it meant to be Jewish. Sometimes motivated by anti-Semitic beliefs, they did not limit their concept of the Jews to those who professed the faith of Judaism and complied with its tenets. In some cases, people who did not consider themselves to be Jewish were labeled Jews just the same. The worst example came when, in 1933, the German Third Reich decreed that a person was Jewish as long as he or she was descended from at least one Jewish parent or grandparent. This was a more expansive interpretation than the traditional Orthodox requirement, which stipulates that a person must be born of a Jewish mother to be Jewish. Of course, the Nazis had their own sinister reasons for expanding this delineation.

There is no doubt that *Jewish* people should determine what it means to be a Jew and to practice Judaism. In fact, Jews have been considering this subject for centuries, and today it remains a point of argument and controversy among Jews. Although it is beyond the scope of any book to decide who is Jewish and who is not, this book will attempt to distill and examine a cogent definition of Judaism.

Judaism teaches that God made an eternal covenant with the descendants of Abraham, Isaac, and Jacob (Israel), and that every Jew participates in this covenant as one of the Chosen People. However, being "chosen" by God does not necessarily impart a notion of superiority.

First and foremost, Judaism is the religion of the Jewish people, wherever they reside. Though over the centuries Jews have dispersed among nations, a strong sense of kinship has remained. This "transnationalism" explains why some Jews feel a connection when introduced to someone else who is also Jewish, experience a sense of pride when a Jew is honored for a major accomplishment, or bear an inordinate sense of loss when learning of something terrible that has befallen a fellow Jew. As Amos Oz, an Israeli writer, observed, "To be a Jew means to feel that wherever a Jew is persecuted for being a Jew—that means you."

Part 1

THE DEVELOPMENT OF JUDAISM

JUDAISM IS A RELIGION STEEPED IN HISTORY. OVER THE COURSE of 4,000 years, what began with the covenant God made with Abraham, the first Jew, evolved through Moses and other Jewish leaders and prophets, all the way to the present. Today, Judaism is a religion with a rich tradition, and several different offshoots have developed. It's important to note that the different branches within Judaism should not be referred to as "denominations." For instance, although there are differences in the respective philosophies of the Orthodox and Reform movements, involving such religious elements as custom, practice, and observance, the differences are not nearly as great as those between and among some Christian denominations. Although throughout history various movements in Judaism have sometimes split off, they have remained different branches growing from the trunk of the same tree.

2

Joseph's saga and the journey to Egypt: The historical context of Passover

Passover celebrates the Jews' Exodus from Egypt, one of the preeminent events in Jewish history. The Passover narrative is recounted in Exodus, the second book of the Torah (the first part of the Hebrew Bible, the five books of Moses). Exodus begins with the death of Joseph and the appearance of a new pharaoh in Egypt. However, it's important to know more about Joseph and exactly how the Hebrews came to be enslaved in Egypt. Without Joseph and his extraordinary adventures, the Hebrews never would have found themselves in Egypt in the first place.

Joseph was the second-youngest son of Jacob (also called Israel), grandson of Isaac and great-grandson of Abraham. Jacob had twelve sons (hence, the twelve tribes of Israel), and Joseph was his favorite. His brothers were jealous, but Joseph did nothing to assuage this jealousy. In fact, he made it worse by doing such things as preening about in his "coat of many colors," a special present from his father. Joseph's jealous brothers wanted to be rid of him, and so they secretly sold him into slavery, telling Jacob that a wild animal had killed Joseph.

Eventually, Joseph became a favored servant to a wealthy Egyptian family. When he rejected the licentious advances of his master's wife, she accused Joseph of attacking her and Joseph soon found himself in prison. While incarcerated, Joseph earned a reputation as an interpreter of dreams. This talent proved useful, and Joseph was summoned to interpret Pharaoh's dreams. Joseph said that Pharaoh's dreams foretold of a great famine, and so he advised Pharaoh on how to prepare for it. When Joseph's prophecy proved true, Pharaoh was grateful and Joseph was given a position of great authority in Egypt.

Meanwhile, the famine ravaged Canaan, the home of Jacob and his family. And so Jacob dispatched his sons to Egypt to buy grain. When they reached their destination, they met with an unexpected surprise, though they did not realize it at first. The person in charge of the grain supplies was none other than their brother Joseph. Once Joseph concluded that his brothers were truly repentant for what they had done to him, he revealed himself, and an emotional family reunion ensued.

Upon hearing that his father was still living, Joseph instructed his brothers to bring him to Egypt. Naturally, Jacob was thrilled to hear that his favorite son was alive. Jacob's entire family gathered all their belongings and made the journey into Egypt, settling in a district known as Goshen.

Though they thrived in Egypt, the Hebrews remained a separate people. They didn't intermarry, and they maintained their identity largely by speaking their own language, wearing distinctive clothing, and giving their children Semitic names.

When Jacob and his clan entered Egypt, they numbered seventy men and women. Since Jacob was also called Israel, his descendants referred to themselves as the Children of Israel. In time, these people became a mighty nation. But their dramatic population growth proved perilous to them in years to come.

— 3 —

The Exodus: Deliverance from slavery in Egypt

Once Joseph died, the Hebrews fell out of favor with Pharaoh. Things no longer boded well for the Hebrews. Their growing numbers threatened the power structure in Egypt. Consequently, in an effort to keep the Hebrew population in check, the Egyptians enslaved them, assigning them harsh work under cruel conditions.

Many scholars believe that Ramses II (1300–1234 or 1347–1280 B.C.E.) was the pharaoh who enslaved the Hebrews. Ramses was known for deploying slave labor to construct his building projects. However, it is likely that Ramses' son, Merneptah, was the pharaoh at the time of the plagues and the Hebrews' exodus from Egypt.

Things became even more precarious for the enslaved Hebrews when astrologers informed Pharaoh that a Hebrew male child born at that time would someday overthrow him. As a result, Pharaoh decreed that every newborn Hebrew male should be drowned in the Nile River.

Not willing to accept the decree as a fait accompli, Moses' parents, Amram and Yochebed, placed their baby boy in a basket and floated him down the Nile River. The boy's sister, Miriam, followed the basket at a safe distance. She watched as Pharaoh's daughter, Bityah, found the basket and lifted it from the river. Little did Miriam know that her brother would ultimately grow up to be the man who defeated Pharaoh.

Bityah called the baby boy Moses (which means "arrived by water").

Moses had a good life growing up as a prince in Pharaoh's palace, but everything changed one day when he saw an Egyptian overseer striking a Hebrew slave. When the overseer would not stop the beating, Moses killed him. Fearing for his life, Moses fled to Midian, where he married Tziporah, the daughter of Jethro, a Midianite priest, and became a shepherd. One day, while tending his flock, Moses came upon a burning bush that was not consumed by the flames. It was then that God spoke to Moses, instructing His reluctant emissary to go into Egypt and tell Pharaoh to free the Hebrews.

Taking his brother Aaron with him for support, Moses conveyed God's demand to Pharaoh. Far from being cooperative, however, Pharaoh was angered, and he made things worse for the Hebrews. Since Pharaoh would not take God's demand seriously, ten plagues were visited upon the Egyptians to demonstrate God's power. These plagues included blood, frogs, lice, wild beasts, pestilence, boils, hail, locusts, darkness, and the slaying of firstborn males.

Before subjecting the Egyptians to the final plague, God directed Moses to instruct each Hebrew family to slaughter an unblemished lamb before sundown. They were to smear the blood of the lamb on doorposts and thresholds and then prepare the lamb for their dinner.

During this meal, the original *seder*, the Hebrews ate the roasted lamb, unleavened bread (because there was not sufficient time for the dough to rise), and maror (bitter herbs). While the Hebrews recounted the many miracles God had performed for them, God passed through Egypt, slaying every firstborn male. Because God passed over the Hebrews' houses, which were marked with the smeared blood of the sacrificial lambs, their sons were spared. Thus, the holiday that celebrates the Jews' eventual liberation from Egypt is known as Passover.

At last, this final plague persuaded Pharaoh to release the Hebrews. The following day, Pharaoh ordered the Hebrews to leave immediately. Under Moses' leadership, the Hebrews departed Egypt. Pharaoh soon regretted his decision, however, and so he sent his army to pursue the Hebrews, catching up with them at the Sea of Reeds (also known as the Red Sea). With the sea directly ahead of them and Pharaoh's mighty army at their backs, the Hebrews were trapped, but God parted the water and allowed them to pass through. When the Egyptian army pursued, they were not so lucky. The water fell back and they all drowned. Gathered together in safety, the Hebrews sang songs of praise to their God (Exodus 15:1–20).

But the Hebrews' trials and tribulations weren't over yet. They wandered in the desert for forty years before entering the Promised Land as a free people.

— 4 —

SCHISM AND REBELLION:
THE HISTORICAL CONTEXT OF HANUKKAH

The story of Hanukkah is a combination of fact and legend, with a little miracle thrown in. To understand the circumstances in which this story took place, a brief history lesson is necessary.

Following the death of King Solomon (c. 997 B.C.E.), the twelve tribes that had comprised the kingdom of Israel split: Israel (consisting of the Ten Tribes) and Judah (comprised of the tribes of Judah and Benjamin). Near the end of the First Temple Era, the Assyrians conquered Israel, and the Ten Tribes were dispersed (hence, the phrase "the Ten Lost Tribes of Israel"). Later, in 586 B.C.E., Babylon conquered the kingdom of Judah and destroyed the First Temple.

After the Babylonian exile, when the Persians conquered the Babylonians, the Persian policy allowed the Judeans to return; many chose to do so and rebuilt the Temple. In 338 B.C.E., Philip of Macedonia successfully invaded Greece. Two years later, after Philip's death, his son, Alexander the Great, conquered territories from Macedonia and Greece to the Persian Empire, including Egypt and Judea.

In Hebrew, the name Judah is "Yehudah," so the people of Judah were called Yehudim. The Greeks used the word Iudea; later, when the Romans replaced the Greeks in control of that part of the world, they changed Iudea to Judea. Thus, these people became known as Judeans and their religion as Judaism.

The Jews did not resist Alexander's army when it arrived in Jerusalem. Alexander was a benevolent ruler who attempted to create a universal culture that blended Greek religions and Eastern philosophy. This culture, known as Hellenism, soon made its presence felt in the hills of Judea.

Many Jews eagerly embraced Hellenism, and it permeated the Jewish community. To these Jews, known as the Hellenists, Greek culture represented the future and success. Many of them spoke Greek as their primary language, especially those in the higher classes, and they even translated the Hebrew Bible into Greek. Furthermore, they abandoned some aspects of Judaism by claiming that only the Written Torah, not the Oral Law, need be followed. (For more on the Written Torah and Oral Law, refer to Part 2.)

On the other hand, many other Jews saw Hellenism as incompatible with Judaism. Although acknowledging the beauty and accomplishments of Greek religion and culture, the Jews who rejected Hellenism believed Greek values to be superficial and inconsistent with Judaism. Judaism and Hellenism were mutually exclusive, they argued.

Thus, a schism developed within the Jewish population. Eventually, the Hellenists became known as the Sadducees, while the reactionary rabbis and priests became known as the Pharisees. (For more on Sadducees and Pharisees, see number 9.) The Sadducees wielded power and money to gain influence with the Greek rulers. Ultimately, they secured control of the high priest position and of the *Sanhedrin* (the highest Jewish court).

—— 5 ——

THE MACCABEAN REBELLION AND
THE RECLAIMING OF THE TEMPLE

When Alexander the Great died, his empire was divided among his generals: Antigonus, Seleucus, and Ptolemy. Ptolemy and his successors, proponents of Hellenism, ruled Egypt and Israel. However, the Ptolemaic dynasty was relatively weak. In 199 B.C.E., Israel came under the control of the Seleucid dynasty. The new government issued decrees that limited the practice of Judaism, including prohibitions on Sabbath (the day of rest) observance, Torah study, and male circumcisions. Violations of these laws were punishable by death. In addition, symbols of the Greek religion and its gods were placed inside the Temple.

In 167 B.C.E., the Greek king Antiochus IV undertook harsher actions in an attempt to force the Jews to adopt Greek practices. His edicts banned all Judaic practices, placed a Hellenist (a Sadducee) in control of the Temple, and desecrated the Temple by requiring the sacrifice of pigs on the altar, and killing those who refused to obey.

The time was ripe for rebellion. The only question was when the kindling would ignite and burst into flames.

Mattityahu (or Mattathias) was an elder and religious leader of the distinguished Hasmonean family, who lived in Modiin when the Greek army arrived to establish a religious altar. Mattityahu received an order to offer a sacrifice to a pagan god, but he refused. Before another Jew, a

Hellenist, could carry out this task, Mattityahu killed him. Turning his fury upon the Greeks, Mattityahu attacked the soldiers. But the first drop of blood spilled in this rebellion for religious freedom was that of a Jew at the hands of another Jew.

Mattityahu and his five sons became known as the Maccabees, which in Hebrew means "men who are as strong as hammers." Though much smaller than the mighty Greek armies, the Jewish forces, under the command of Judah Maccabee, ultimately triumphed. On the twenty-fifth day of the month of Kislev (the first day of Hanukkah), the Maccabees reclaimed the Temple. It was a victory of the oppressed over the oppressors.

— 6 —

Exile in Persia: The historical context of Purim

The tale of Purim takes place 2,500 years ago, after the destruction of the First Temple, when the Jews lived in exile in Babylon. The events recounted in the Purim narrative may or may not be authentic. Some scholars hold that Purim is a carryover from a pagan carnival held during the Babylonian New Year celebration. The carnival was an occasion filled with dancing and mirthmaking, and many Jews could not restrain themselves from joining in the merriment. Realizing that any prohibition to participate would be fruitless, the rabbis added some Jewish flavor to the affair and rewrote it as the Esther/Mordecai/Haman legend.

Some secular scholars have also theorized that the Purim story might possibly have another historical basis apart from what is recounted in the book of Esther. There might have been an attempt to murder the Jewish population during the reign of Xerxes (485–465 B.C.E.) or Artaxerxes II (403–358 B.C.E.).

However, such conjectures are no more or less likely than the possibility that the story of Purim (or some variation thereof) did, in fact, occur. Either way, Purim has become an integral part of the Jewish tradition. Jews have been observing Purim for more than two millennia, which makes it noteworthy, regardless of whether or not the historical event actually took place.

At the time of the Jews' exile in Persia, the court of King Ahasuerus celebrated the expansion of the Babylonian empire with a six-month feast. Although Jewish rabbis forbade the Jews from participating, most Jews joined in the festivities. During one of the many feasts, the tipsy Ahasuerus sent for his queen, Vashti, to appear at the party. For whatever reason—one version has it that she was too modest to dance in front of the king and his company; another suggests she was vain and didn't want to appear because of a blemish on her face—Vashti refused to oblige. This refusal cost Vashti her life.

Seeking a new queen, Ahasuerus staged a beauty contest, and he picked Esther as a winner. Though Jewish, Esther followed the advice of her uncle and guardian, Mordecai—keeping her Jewish identity to herself, she married King Ahasuerus.

Incidentally, Esther's real Hebrew name was Hadassah. But the Persians at the King's court called her Esther, comparing her to the divinity known as Ishtar/Astarte/Easter, who was the personification of beauty in their eyes. Another possibility is that the word *esther* came from the Hebrew root that means "hidden"—a major motif in the Purim story.

At any rate, soon after Esther married the king, Mordecai uncovered a plot to assassinate Ahasuerus. Although he thwarted the conspiracy, he was not rewarded.

Meanwhile, an ambitious and ruthless advisor named Haman stepped into the spotlight when King Ahasuerus appointed him chief minister. Haman issued a proclamation that all must bow before him. When Mordecai refused to prostrate himself before Haman (because Jews are forbidden to bow to any person or icon), he incurred Haman's enmity. The best way to dispose of Mordecai, Haman concluded, was to get rid of him and his entire tribe. Having convinced Ahasuerus that the Jews were a strange and separate people who posed an internal threat, Haman obtained the king's permission to have them slaughtered.

The king issued a secret decree authorizing the populace to rise up and murder the Jews. The day of the genocide was established by "the casting of lots" (*purim* in Hebrew—hence, the name of the holiday), and it was set as the thirteenth day of *Adar*. Everything was in place for the massacre of Persia's Jews.

7

ESTHER MAKES HER CASE AND THE JEWS PREVAIL

When Mordecai learned that the Persians had marked his people for slaughter, he enlisted his niece Esther's help, beseeching her to plead their case to Ahasuerus. After some vacillation, Esther agreed.

Esther fasted and prayed for three days, paid a visit to the king, and then invited both Ahasuerus and Haman to a special banquet. Haman construed the invitation as a sign of royal favor. Sure of his power and thinking that revenge was close at hand, Haman ordered that gallows be erected to hang Mordecai.

Meanwhile, King Ahasuerus remembered the time when Mordecai revealed the assassination plot and realized that Mordecai was never rewarded for it. At the banquet, Ahasuerus asked Haman how a man who saved the king's life should be compensated. Haman, thinking the king was referring to none other than himself, suggested lavish gifts and honors. The king agreed, and much to his dismay, Haman discovered that he had to reward Mordecai.

Then, when Ahasuerus asked Esther what she would like from him, she made her request—she wanted the king to spare her life and the lives of her people. The perplexed sovereign did not understand, and so Queen Esther explained that because the royal edict called for the death of the Jewish people, it called for her death, too, because she was a Jew.

Ahasuerus was furious with Haman, and he ordered that Haman and his sons be hanged—on the very same gallows Haman had erected for Mordecai. After the king appointed Mordecai as his new chief minister, Moredecai set out to thwart Haman's plot. Although the original decree could not be rescinded, the king authorized Mordecai to issue another decree that would allow the Jews to defend themselves.

On the day of the attack, those who chose to rise up against the Jews were met with fierce resistance. The Persian mobs were vanquished, and the Jews prevailed. What would have been a day of tragedy in Jewish history instead became a day of jubilation. The following day, the Jews rejoiced and celebrated their deliverance.

— 8 —

Branches of Judaism under Greek and Roman rule

No examination of Judaism's growth would be complete without considering the development of its various branches, and you'll learn more about those toward the end of Part 1. Before studying Judaism's contemporary movements, however, it's important to understand Judaism's divisions in the past. No one can say with any certainty when the first formal divisions within Judaism arose. The oldest records we have of an explicit difference of opinion took place during the time of the Maccabean Revolution, in the second century B.C.E. (For more on the Maccabean Revolution, see number 5.)

During the period leading up to the Maccabean rebellion, the Jews lived under Greek occupation. As previously mentioned, the Greeks were an enlightened people who were tolerant of their subjects. As a result, secular life was good and a number of Jews were attracted to Greek culture, known as Hellenism.

Hellenism, with its pagan joy, freedom, and love of life, stood in stark contrast to traditional Judaism's austere morality and monotheism. Those Jews who allowed themselves to be influenced by Hellenism were known as Hellenistic Jews; the Hasideans (not to be confused with Hasids, who you will learn about at the end of Part 1) formed their conservative opposition.

While the tension between the two groups sometimes led to violence, the situation resolved itself because the happy freedom the Jews enjoyed during this period didn't last. As fate would have it, the Greeks began to oppress the Jews, and when faced with an external enemy, the Jews united in their fight for independence. (This era in Jewish history, which the holiday Hanukkah commemorates, will be discussed in greater detail in Part 4.)

By the time Rome later conquered the land of ancient Israel, Judaism had split into at least three distinct sects. The Essenes formed an ascetic and mystical order, consisting mostly of adult males who took an oath of celibacy. These members pledged piety toward God, justice to men, and adherence to their order and its doctrines. Ceremonial purity and the wearing of white garments were common.

The Essenes accepted the authenticity of several men who claimed to be messiahs. This ardent belief in the true messiah's imminent arrival may have played a role in Christianity's emergence. However, the sect disappeared sometime in the second century C.E., due to the Essenes' practice of celibacy, lack of new converts, and the rise of some forms of Christianity that incorporated certain aspects of the Essene worldview.

The Sadducees embraced some of the Hellenistic elements that were previously incorporated into Judaism during Greek rule. Their relatively small following included the priests and the upper class of Jewish society. The Sadducees did not believe in the Oral Torah, and their interpretation of the Written Torah was narrow and conservative. Since so many priests were a part of this movement, it's no surprise that the Temple in Jerusalem was the center of their worship. Consequently, when the Romans destroyed the Temple in 70 C.E., this sect disappeared.

Pharisees formed the third and most powerful group. The Pharisees believed that both the Written and Oral Torah came directly from God and were, therefore, valid and binding. Because of their disagreements with the Sadducees, who had control of the Temple, the Pharisees developed the synagogue as an alternative place for study and worship. Their liturgy consisted of biblical and prophetic readings and the repetition of the *Shema* (Judaism's central prayer).

In accordance with the Torah, the Pharisees began to codify the *Halakah* (the Law), insisting upon its strict observance. However, they did encourage debate among scholars about the finer points of the law, and they also emphasized the individual's relationship to God. It should also be mentioned that a fourth subgroup existed during the time of the

Roman Empire. The movement of Zealots did not really represent a division. Rather, it was a nationalistic movement, "zealous" in seeking independence from Rome. Members of this group did not survive the war with Rome and, like the Essenes and Sadducees, lost influence after the destruction of the Temple and the suppression of the Jewish revolt.

The Pharisaic movement alone endured the rebellion against Rome. And until almost the end of the first millennium C.E., no other separate movements within Judaism would emerge. Naturally, such a state of affairs could not be expected to last forever.

9

THE DIFFERENCE BETWEEN KARAITIC, ASHKENAZIC, AND SEPHARDIC JEWS

The major disagreement between the Pharisees and the Sadducees was the validity of the Oral Torah and whether or not it had come directly from God or was merely commentary inspired by human minds alone (as discussed in number 16). During the ninth century C.E., a movement in Persia again voiced skepticism over the validity of the Oral Torah, rejecting rabbinical law as part of the Jewish tradition. The Karaites, or "People of the Scripture," believed in a literal reading of the Bible without rabbinical interpretation. The Rabbanites (Rabbinical Judaism) opposed this viewpoint.

It has been estimated that, at one time, as many as 40 percent of Jews were Karaites. Until recently, a surviving Karaite community existed in Egypt. In 1967, after the Six-Day War between Egypt and Israel, most Karaites immigrated to Israel, Europe, or the United States. Currently, the Karaite community is minuscule, but it retains its particular culture, which developed during centuries of existence in Egypt.

Today, most Jews either identify themselves as Ashkenazic or Sephardic. Their differences are the result of history and geography. The Babylonian exile and later dispersions forced the Jews to live in the Diaspora (communities outside of Israel). Those who eventually ended up in Central and Eastern Europe became known as Ashkenazim, or Ashkenazic Jews (derived from *Ashkenaz*, the Hebrew word for "Germany"). Those who resided in southern France, Spain, Portugal, North Africa, and the Middle East came to be known as Sephardim, or Sephardic Jews (derived from *Sepharad*, the Hebrew word for "Spain").

Most of the early Jewish settlers in the United States were Sephardic, as were the first Jewish synagogues (Shearith Israel, founded in New York in 1684, and Congregation Mikveh Israel, founded in Philadelphia in 1740). However, the majority of Jews living in the United States today are Ashkenazic. They are descended from Jews who emigrated from Germany and Eastern Europe from the mid-nineteenth through the early twentieth centuries.

The respective cultures of the countries in which the Ashkenazim and the Sephardim lived greatly affected these two Jewish groups in terms of their customs, language, and modes of thinking. It has been said that perhaps Sephardic Jews place greater emphasis on intellectualism, although they also practiced the Kabbalah, a form of Jewish mysticism (see number 31 for more on the Kabalah) Unlike the Ashkenazim, the Sephardim never split into separate branches of Judaism. Today, Sephardim practice Orthodox Judaism, which is similar to the Orthodox branch of the Ashkenazim.

— 10 —

ORTHODOX JUDAISM

During the last millennium and up until the nineteenth century, the Orthodox branch of Judaism was by far the most prevalent. In most places, in fact, it was the only type of Judaism that existed. While there was some diversity within the Orthodox branch—between the Sephardim and the Ashkenazim (see number 14 and 15 to learn about the diversity among the Ashkenazim and between the Hasidim and the mitnagdim)—the theology among the different groups was essentially the same. What ultimately did lead to divisions within Judaism were the differing perceptions about the Halakah (the laws and rules Jews are obliged to follow) and the Torah.

The essential principle governing Orthodox Judaism is *Torah min Hashamayim*. This means that the Torah, both Written Law (Scriptures) and Oral Law (rabbinic interpretation and commentaries), is conclusive.

It is directly derived from God and must be obeyed. Orthodox Jews lead a *mitzvah*-centered life. There is not much room for individual discretion regarding which mitzvot (commandments to be fulfilled) need to be obeyed or how they should be practiced.

Synagogue services are conducted in Hebrew, and men and women sit separately. Women are not ordained as rabbis, nor do they count in a *minyan* (the group of ten necessary for public prayer in Jewish tradition). While the synagogue is the domain of men, women clearly have dominion over the home. The tasks of following *kashrut* (dietary laws) and the mitzvot concerning *Shabbat* (the Sabbath) largely fall upon Orthodox females. In addition, women are primarily responsible for ritual purity and for faithfully upholding the laws of *niddah* (regarding the separation of a husband and wife during the wife's menstrual period).

Today, several different groups within Orthodox Judaism share common fundamental beliefs. The best known of these groups is probably the ultra-Orthodox, which includes the Hasidim. These Jews obey Halakah in a closed society, where the entire community follows the same observances and rituals. This is not as difficult as doing so while living in an open society where the prevalent customs and habits are different. It is easy to close your business on Saturday for Shabbat in a community where no business would be conducted that day in any event. This explains why many ultra-Orthodox communities, particularly the Hasidim, are so insular.

By contrast, the modern Orthodox are integrated in contemporary society while still observing Halakic laws. Modern Orthodox must be consistently vigilant in maintaining a balance as they live and work in contemporary society.

When Jews were segregated in ghettos or the "pale of settlement" (regions in Russia that were designated for Jews to inhabit), they had no access to secular society. Therefore, they led their lives according to the customs that had been practiced for generations before them.

As the Enlightenment spread through Europe in the seventeenth and eighteenth centuries, many societies began to open at least some of their doors to Jews. Suddenly, particularly after the effects of emancipation in Germany in the nineteenth century, Jews had choices and alternatives. They had access to new ideas and new occupations; the barriers that had encased their closed society were broken down.

Strict observance of Halakah made integrating into secular society difficult, if not outright impossible. Moreover, many Jews incorporated aspects of the Enlightenment into their own way of thinking. The concept of divinely revealed commandments and the stress on ethnocentricity ran contrary to so-called enlightened ideas. Such were the circumstances that brought forth Reform Judaism, as you will see in number 11.

11

REFORM JUDAISM

Reform Judaism—sometimes known as Liberal or Progressive Judaism—had its beginnings in nineteenth-century Germany, where the Jews of the time coined the insightful phrase "German in the streets; Jewish in the home." This reflected the Jewish people's desire to take advantages of the new opportunities afforded by an open and liberal society.

The first reforms introduced to Judaism were not initiated in the home, however; they occurred in the synagogue. In the early nineteenth century, several German congregations instituted fundamental changes in the Jewish service, including mixed-gender seating, a shortened service, use of the vernacular in the liturgy, single-day observance of holidays, and the inclusion of musical instruments and a choir.

American Reform Judaism was born when some of these German reformers immigrated to the United States in the mid-nineteenth century. Some of the first Reform congregations in the United States were Beth Elohim in Charleston, South Carolina (1825); Har Sinai in Baltimore, Maryland (1842); Bene Yeshurun (I. M. Wise) in Cincinnati, Ohio (1854); Adath Israel (The Temple) in Louisville, Kentucky (1885); and Keneseth Israel in Philadelphia, Pennsylvania (1856).

Under the leadership of Rabbi Isaac Mayer Wise, Reform Judaism became the dominant belief held by American Jews. By 1880, over 90 percent of American synagogues were Reform. Although this situation would change with the arrival of the first waves of Eastern European immigrants, who were predominantly Orthodox, today Reform Judaism is still the largest movement.

Some American congregations went beyond the German Reform movement's alterations. A number of congregations became almost indistinguishable from neighboring Protestant churches, singing hymns and, in some cases, even holding Shabbat services on Sunday! However, by the 1930s the Reform movement gradually returned to a more traditional approach.

The essential principles of Reform Judaism suggest that religion ought to be dynamic and that the essence of Judaism lies in its ethical teachings. In contrast to Orthodox tenets, Reform Jews believe that while the Torah was divinely inspired, it was written by a number of individuals, and then revised and edited. Therefore, while Reform Jews revere and retain most of the Torah's values and ethics, each individual is free to follow those practices that are most likely to advance a meaningful and ethical life and enhance his or her relationship with God.

Although Reform Judaism offers room for individualism, it does have fundamental principles, including these beliefs:

- The Torah was divinely inspired but authored by humans.
- There is only one God.
- The reinterpretation of Torah is continuous and must be adapted for new circumstances and challenges.
- The moral and ethical components in the Torah are important.
- The sexes are to be treated equally.

It should come as no surprise that, given its more egalitarian view of males and females, Reform Judaism ordains female rabbis and cantors. Moreover, because Reform Judaism places such emphasis on equality, this branch of Judaism is involved in social action for many worthy causes.

In recent years, Reform Judaism has experienced an increased movement toward spirituality and conventional ritual. In response, Reform has adopted a more traditional stance concerning certain practices. For example, it allows, and even encourages, the wearing of *kippot* (yarmulkes or skullcaps) and *tallit* (ceremonial shawls men wear at religious services). Reform Judaism has also brought Hebrew back into its prayer books. And there hasn't been a Shabbat service on a Sunday in decades.

12

CONSERVATIVE JUDAISM

Although the Reform movement of the nineteenth century had many supporters, some Jews felt Reform Judaism went too far. A more reasoned and less extreme break from Orthodox Judaism seemed desirable. Hence, Conservative Judaism was born.

In 1845, Rabbi Zecharias Frankel broke with the emerging European Reform movement in Germany when he insisted that the liturgy should be conducted in Hebrew. A decade later, Rabbi Frankel became the first head of the Jewish Theological Seminary of Breslau.

The seeds of Conservative Judaism were sown in the United States with the founding of the Jewish Theological Seminary of America in 1886. However, Conservative Judaism did not really begin to expand until Dr. Solomon Schechter became president of the seminary in 1902. In 1913, Dr. Schechter organized the movement under the aegis of the United Synagogue of Conservative Judaism. Today, the Conservative Judaism movement is nearly as large as Reform Judaism.

Like Reform Jews, Conservatives believe that the Torah was divinely inspired but authored by humans. Conservative Judaism parts with Reform in that it generally accepts the binding nature of Halakah. However, Conservatives do agree with Reform that Halakah is subject to change and that adaptations may be made based on the contemporary culture so long as the Halakah remains true to Judaism's values.

Conservative Judaism's most notable accomplishment is in the area of synagogue services. It has offered a middle ground for Jews who are not satisfied with either the Orthodox or the Reform approach. In the Conservative service, Hebrew is the predominant language, but the worshippers' native language is used as well. Conservative congregations allow men and women to sit together, and many also have choirs and organs.

Conservative Judaism's positions vary between liberal and traditional. Since 1983, women have been accepted for training in the rabbinate. On the other hand, Conservative Judaism has reaffirmed matrilineal descent in determining who is a Jew. It is expected that Shabbat and dietary laws be observed, although many if not most Conservative Jews either do not adhere to these mitzvot or follow them to a limited extent.

At present, an estimated 23 percent of all synagogues in the United States are part of the Conservative branch. There are more than 850 Conservative synagogues nationwide as well as many more in Canada, and Conservative Jews number approximately 1.5 million worldwide.

In general, there is a great deal of variability among today's Conservative practices. Some seem almost indistinguishable from Reform congregations, while others come close to the Orthodox service.

— 13 —

THE EMERGENCE OF RECONSTRUCTIONISM IN TWENTIETH-CENTURY AMERICA

Reconstructionism is distinct from the Orthodox, Reform, and Conservative movements for two reasons. First, it does not fit as neatly along the spectrum of observance as do the other three branches; that is, it cannot be differentiated merely by degrees of adherence to the Halakah. Second, Reconstructionism is a movement based on the teachings of just one man, its philosopher and founder, Mordecai M. Kaplan (1881–1983).

Reconstructionism, Judaism's youngest movement, took shape in twentieth-century America. Although the Jewish Reconstructionist Federation was founded in 1955, Reconstructionism did not become the fourth branch of American Judaism until the late 1960s, when it was able to train its own rabbis at the Reconstructionist Rabbinical College.

The seed for Reconstructionism germinated from an article Mordecai Kaplan wrote in 1920. He called for a reinterpreting of Judaism in keeping with modern thought and strengthening ties with Jewish communities in Palestine. Two years later, as he became more vocal in urging economic justice and more critical of orthodoxy, he resigned from the pulpit of a Conservative congregation in Manhattan. Leaving with thirty-five families, he founded a congregation based on his philosophy of Judaism, known as the Society for the Advancement of Judaism (SAJ).

During the first two decades of its existence, the SAJ remained affiliated with the Conservative movement. However, in 1963, when Kaplan retired from teaching at the Jewish Theological Seminary, a Conservative organization, the road was paved for the founding of an institution that would train Reconstructionist rabbis. Five years later, the Reconstructionist Rabbinical College was established.

Kaplan had no desire to create a new branch of Judaism, but given his unique philosophy, this was inevitable. By the 1970s, Reconstructionism was recognized as the fourth branch on the Judaic tree. It remains the smallest movement, with 100 congregations worldwide, but, given Kaplan's legacy and the philosophy his followers developed, its impact belies its numbers.

Reconstructionism is a revolutionary concept. It rejects the notion that the Jews alone are God's "chosen people." Each culture and civilization, Kaplan postulated, has a unique contribution to make to the greater human community. Judaism is only one of these cultures.

Furthermore, Halakah need only be observed if an individual

chooses to do so; if a person does follow an aspect of Halakah, it should not be because it is binding law from God, but because it is a valuable cultural remnant. In fact, in Reconstructionism the entire notion of a supernatural God acting in history is discarded. Instead, God is considered to be a process or power—an expression of the highest values and ideals of a civilization.

Kaplan taught that Judaism is more than a religion. It's an evolving religious civilization that incorporates traditions, laws, customs, language, literature, music, and art. While he believed in the need for all Jewish communities to thrive in the Diaspora, Kaplan foresaw a Jewish state as the hub of the Jewish wheel. Therefore, Zionism and Israel's establishment have always been fundamental to Reconstructionism.

Although Reconstructists' social ideas are quite liberal, their services are more conservative. Except for the fact that men and women sit together and that women can be ordained as rabbis, you might think you are *davening* (reciting Jewish prayers) in a modern-Orthodox *shul* (Yiddish for "synagogue"). Reconstructionism observes traditional practices and recognizes kashrut, the Shabbat and the holidays, the liturgy, and life-cycle events. It also places emphasis on learning that does not end with a bar or bat mitzvah but continues through adulthood.

One point often puzzles those who learn about Reconstructionism. If it does not teach belief in a God who acts in history, why the prayers and traditional liturgy? That answer may be found in the Jewish concept of prayer. To learn more about the role of prayer, refer to Part 3.

——— 14 ———

THE SCHISM BETWEEN MYSTICS AND TRADITIONALISTS, AND THE BEGINNING OF HASIDISM

Probably no group in Judaism underscores the encounter with God in the world more than the Hasidim. Although some people see Hasidism as a branch of Judaism, it is really a spiritual movement. This movement's emergence represented a deep schism within Judaism during the eighteenth and nineteenth centuries. Those who opposed Hasidism became known as *mitnagdim*, or "opponents."

While Hasidism still has its detractors today, they are generally neither organized nor vociferous in their condemnation. The original mitnagdim who adhered to traditional rabbinical Judaism are now more or less at one with the Hasidim in their rejection of Judaism's more liberal movements. Simply put, the Hasidim are practitioners of a form of mystical Orthodox Judaism. All Hasidim are Orthodox, but not all Orthodox are Hasidim.

The Hasidic movement emerged from one of the darker pages of Jewish history, during the times of the Cossack massacres of 1648 led by Bogdan Chmielnicki. Thousands of Jews (about half the Jewish population of Ukraine and Poland) were murdered, and hundreds of Jewish communities were destroyed. Well into the eighteenth century, Eastern European Jewry suffered regular acts of violence and discrimination.

During such times, it is common for people to seek salvation and solace wherever they can find it. Many Jews came to prefer the spiritual nature of the Kabbalah to the legalistic approach of Orthodox Judaism. In reaction, rabbinic studies became even more focused on Halakah and conventional Talmud rumination.

As another consequence of these trying times, there was a tendency to embrace "saviors." Hence, in the seventeenth century many Jews flocked around a Turkish Jew, named Shabbetai Zvi, believed to be a messiah. Later in the eighteenth century, Jacob Frank, a Polish messianic pretender, garnered a large following. As with all false messiahs, disillusionment ensued when Shabbetai Zvi adopted Islam and Jacob Frank converted to Christianity.

Since these false messiahs drew their support from the lower and less-educated classes of the Jewish population—where mysticism (and even magic) were practiced—the educated classes grew wary and intolerant of those who would not strictly adhere to traditional ways. A schism between the mystics and the traditionalists was in the makings.

Out of this schism emerged Rabbi Israel ben Eliezer, who became known as the *Ba'al Shem Tov* (Master of the Good Name). The Ba'al Shem Tov was born around 1700 in Ukraine. He was a simple man who roamed the countryside, believing that there he could best commune with God (much like Abraham and the early nomadic Hebrews did in the desert). His appeal was widespread because he criticized the pedantic reiterations of Jewish scholars and the rabbinical emphasis on formal learning. His movement became known as Hasidism and his followers were called Hasidim. Despite his followers' fervent devotion, the Ba'al Shem Tov shunned any claim to being a messiah.

Ultimately, the Ba'al Shem Tov (also known by the abbreviation "Besht") settled in a remote Carpathian village where he supported his family by digging lime. Teaching in parables and recounting simple stories, the Besht gained widespread appeal, despite public denunciation from the rabbinical establishment, which claimed that he was ignorant and irreverent.

One of the more revealing stories about the Besht and his teachings has to do with the time he refused to enter a house of prayer. "I cannot enter there," said the Besht. "The house is full to the brim of teaching and prayer." This puzzled his companions, since what the Besht said seemed to be a compliment. Seeing their bewildered faces, the Besht went on to explain: "During the day, the people speak here words without true devotion, without love and compassion, words that have no wings. They remain between the walls, they squat on the floor, they grow layer by layer like decaying leaves until the decay has packed the house to overflowing and there is no longer room for me in there."

When asked to explain Hasidism, the Besht replied: "Do you know the story of the ironmonger who wanted to become independent? He bought an anvil, a hammer and bellows and went to work. Nothing happened—the forge remained inert. Then an old ironmonger . . . told him, 'You have everything you need except the spark.' That is what Hasidism is: the spark."

From this Hasidic tale, you can glean the importance of sincerity in the hierarchy of Hasidic values. The moral here is that *how* you pray is more important than *where* you pray. Sincerity is required not only in prayer but in all of life's actions. And herein lies the essence of Hasidism as expressed by the Besht himself.

It's that same spark of the Divine presence within all of us, every living creature and every thing. It is the purpose of the Hasid to redeem these sparks. According to what the Ba'al Shem Tov taught, this is not accomplished through perfunctory prayer or asceticism but through *kavana* (pure intention), *devekut* (clinging, devotion to God's presence), joy in performing all deeds, and sincere prayer. The goal is to hallow life and thus awaken the holy reality in all things.

When the Besht died in 1760, he left behind no written work of his own. However, the principles the Besht established remain the core of Hasidism even now.

—— 15 ——

HASIDIC PRACTICES TODAY

After the Besht died, there was no formal framework for Hasidic leadership. At first, his circle of disciples, each considered a *tzaddik* (a righteous one), exercised the Besht's authority. Since the average Hasid could not be expected to achieve full religious perfection, he would devote himself to a particular tzaddik and obtain vicarious fulfillment through him. The different Hasidic sects can trace their roots to a specific tzaddik and often to a town or city in Eastern Europe.

Through the early twentieth century, Hasidic populations were largely confined to Eastern Europe. The devastation these communities suffered during World War II was unimaginable. Yet Hasidism survived, and new communities were established in the United States, Israel, Canada, and other parts of the world.

These communities are often identified by the name of the geographic locale where their forebears resided in Europe, and they are centered on their own *rebbe*, or "spiritual master." Some of these sects are fairly well known, such as the Lubavitcher (Chabad), Satmar, Breslov, and Modsitzer, but there are many more, each with its own customs, style of service, philosophy, and politics. Generally, however, Hasidic groups share much in common. They revere the Besht and other tzaddikim, and they have similar customs of dress. The men wear *payees* (side earlocks), full beards, hats, and dark clothes. The *tzitzit* (white tassels) are attached to the *tallit katan* (a small prayer shawl), also known as *arba kanfot* (four corners). Hasidic men wear the arba kanfot throughout the day underneath their clothes. Women wear modest dresses; married women wear scarves or other head coverings. (It is a common practice for married women to wear wigs.)

In the mid-twentieth century, the philosopher Martin Buber translated numerous Hasidic tales that were subsequently published. Buber's own philosophy of "I and Thou" has striking parallels with Hasidism and Jewish mysticism. It is something worth investigating more deeply if you are looking for a more "secular" approach to Jewish spirituality.

Part 2
ESSENTIAL BELIEFS
AND LAWS

FOR CENTURIES, JEWS HAVE BEEN CALLED THE "PEOPLE of the Book." Religious study has always been revered in the Jewish tradition, and there is much to study, including the Torah, Talmud, the Midrash, and other important texts, which will be explained in this section.

Yet Judaism is a religion that goes beyond the system of spiritual beliefs set forth in these holy texts. It also speaks to practical concerns of everyday living and human conduct, entering into the very marrow of daily existence.

The Jewish faith encompasses a vast system of laws so detailed that there is not an aspect of human life it doesn't touch upon. Why the need for such extensive laws? Read on, and you'll begin to understand Jewish devotion to the Torah and its rules, as well as the whys and whats covered in the collection of Jewish laws known as the Halakah.

But there is much more to Judaism than just mundane rules and regulations. Jewish spirituality and mysticism, in the form of Kabbalah and Hasidism, are just as much a part of this religious tradition as devotion to the Torah and the keeping of all the laws prescribed by the Halakah.

16

THE TORAH: JUDAISM'S CORNERSTONE

Sometimes called the Hebrew or Holy Scriptures, the Torah is the first part of the Bible. The Bible is also known by the acronym "TaNaKH" (or Tanach), formed from the first letter of each of the three sections of the Bible: *Torah*, *Nevi'im* (Prophets), and *Ketuvim* (Writings). If you are not Jewish, keep in mind that you should avoid referring to the Holy (Hebrew) Bible as the "Old Testament." What Christians call the "New Testament" is not part of Jewish scripture. Consequently, there can be nothing "old" about the Hebrew Bible.

The Torah is Judaism's cornerstone. The word *Torah* is sometimes translated as "the Law." It also means "a teaching" because it represents God's instructions regarding how Jews should live and what they ought to believe.

The Torah is comprised of two components: the Written Torah, *Torah Shebichtav*, and the Oral Torah, *Torah Sheb'al Peh*. In its most limited sense, the Torah comprises the five books of Moses, also called the *Pentateuch*. However, in its broadest sense, Torah encompasses everything that follows the Pentateuch—the whole body of Jewish law and teachings.

The Written Torah contains twenty-four books in all, divided into three parts. As the first part of the Written Torah, the five books of Moses, or *Chumash*, include *B'reishit* (Genesis), *Shemot* (Exodus), *Vayikra* (Leviticus), *Bamidbar* (Numbers), and *Devarim* (Deuteronomy).

The second part of the Written Torah, *Nevi'im* (Prophets), contains eight books: *Yehoshua* (Joshua), *Shoftim* (Judges), *Shmuel* (Samuel I and II), *Melachim* (Kings I and II), *Yirmiyahu* (Jeremiah), *Yechezkel* (Ezekiel), *Yeshayahu* (Isaiah), and *Trey Asar* (the Twelve). This last book encompasses the remaining twelve prophets: Hosea, Joel, Amos, Obadiah, Jonah, Micah, Nahum, Habakkuk, Zephaniah, Haggai, Zachariah, and Malachi.

Finally, the third part of the Written Torah, the Ketuvim, consists of eleven books: *Tehillim* (Psalms), *Mishlei* (Proverbs), *Iyov* (Job), *Shir Ha-Shirim* (Song of Songs), *Ruth, Eichah* (Lamentations), *Kohelet* (Ecclesiastes), *Esther, Daniel, Ezra* and *Nechemiah,* and *Divrei Ha-Yamim* (Chronicles).

The Jewish tradition teaches that in addition to giving Moses the Written Torah, God also provided explanations—the Oral Torah. These unwritten exegeses were meant to be passed from teacher to student.

Maybe you're beginning to wonder just how God imparted this immense information to the Jews. Perhaps you've heard the story that God whispered the additional 613 commandments into Moses' ear. Remember that people use these sorts of anthropomorphic features to explain divine happenings in terms to which human beings can relate. Such stories are there to help us understand how God acted in history and communed with mortals. But who is to say what means of communication God really employed? Perhaps it was something more akin to inspiration, intuition, or ESP.

The point is that according to traditional Jewish stories, God transmitted the Torah to His chosen people through Moses. Beginning around 200 C.E., the Oral Torah was inscribed into a series of books called the

Mishna. In Judaism, it is axiomatic that the Torah is everlasting and immutable. Since Torah comes from God and God is eternal, it follows that the Torah also shares this feature.

Undoubtedly, this is one reason Judaism stresses the responsibility of being true to the Torah and maintaining it as part of the Jews' very existence. According to Judaism, God chose the Hebrews for the task of receiving and preserving the Torah, and this task cannot be abrogated.

Keep in mind, that Judaism is a vibrant religion that deals with the application of the Law to everyday life. New thoughts, new questions, new ideas, and new answers are always taking shape as scholars study the Torah and its precepts are applied. This has given rise to other great works that also play an integral role in Judaism.

17

THE TALMUD: APPLYING THE LAWS OF THE BIBLE TO LIFE

In the years following the destruction of the Second Temple (70 C.E.), scholars and jurists wanted to ensure that the Oral Law, passed down from teacher to student, would not be forgotten. In order to do so, a group led by Rabbi Yehuda Ha-Nasi assembled a basic outline of Oral Law's contents. Known as the *Mishna*, this work was completed around 200 C.E.

But students and scholars of the Torah had far from completed their work. Over the next several hundred years, they continued to raise questions and seek explanations for the text and its laws. Once again, to keep the results of their efforts from being lost, Rav Ashi, a teacher and scholar who reestablished the Jewish academy at Sura (in ancient Babylonia), and his student/assistant Ravina guided the compilation of the *Gemara*, the collection of rabbis' commentaries on the Mishna from the third through fifth centuries C.E. Together, the Mishna and Gemara form what is known as the *Talmud*.

There are actually two Talmuds—the Jerusalem Talmud and the Babylonian Talmud. Generally, when people speak of the Talmud, however, they are referring to the more comprehensive of the two, the Babylonian Talmud.

The Talmud is a record of the way rabbis, scholars, and jurists have applied the laws of the Bible to all of the things they faced in the course of their daily lives. Themes include the social and the private; urban and rural; civil and criminal; public and domestic; everyday and ritual.

The Talmud is divided into six sections called *sedarim* ("orders"), or *seder* when referring to just one. Each seder contains several books called *masekhtot* ("tractates"); there are sixty-three masekhtot. Although the respective sedarim (not to be confused with the Passover Seder) seem to address narrow topics, each seder actually contains diverse subjects.

The six sedarim are as follows:

1. Zera'im (seeds): This seder deals primarily with agricultural laws but also laws of prayer and blessings; it is comprised of eleven masekhtot.

2. Mo'ed (season): This seder addresses Shabbat and festivals; it includes twelve masekhtot.
3. Nashim (women): This seder deals with the laws of marriage and divorce; it contains seven masekhtot.
4. Nezikin (damages): This seder deals with civil law and ethics; it contains ten masekhtot.
5. Kodashim (holy things): Sacrifices and the Temple are considered in this seder, which includes eleven masekhtot.
6. Toharot (purities): This seder deals with laws of ritual purity and impurity, and contains twelve masekhtot.

The Talmud is the written product of discussions among a number of learned authors—but it is so much more. Although it deals with legalisms and extremely specific issues, it is not a code or catechism that lays down the law in summary, categorical form. The Talmud is filled with legend, folklore, parables, reminiscences, prayers, theology, and theosophy.

The Talmud is the end result of a process through which the law is made clear. Hence, the tensions, conflicts, and arguments of its collaborators come alive before the reader's eyes. If you examine a page in the Talmud, you'll see that a statement is quoted, immediately followed by scholars' and sages' exchanges, meant to explain the "text." These explications are the most important parts of the Talmud.

As a result, delving into the Talmud is not like reading a book of laws. Rather, it gives the reader a glimpse of the living, breathing people who left a little of themselves dispersed throughout the pages.

Today, many observant Jews study a page of the Talmud every day. This practice, referred to as *daf yomi*, was started at the First International Congress of the Agudath Yisrael World Movement in 1923. Many synagogues organize less rigorous classes or informal sessions that allow participants to study the Talmud together.

—— 18 ——

USING THE RESPONSA TRADITION TO ANSWER CONTEMPORARY QUESTIONS

As noted in number 17, the Jewish tradition has a history of examining the problems and issues of daily life, and then applying the laws of the Bible to them. By the Middle Ages, volumes of text had been written to provide authority upon which the rabbis could rely in answering questions regarding the Jews' daily lives.

In times past, the Jews often sought guidance from their rabbi on matters of everyday life, ritual, and tradition. When local rabbis faced difficult issues in applying Jewish law to specific circumstances, they often wrote to the most respected rabbis to seek guidance. These queries included the particulars of each matter, references to the applicable Talmudic passages involved, and the rabbi's own interpretation.

In turn, the response of the rabbi whose opinion had been sought would include the basis for his conclusion and a reasoned argument to substantiate it. Over the years, these responsa *(teshuvot)* were collected into printed volumes, providing even more material to be read and studied.

The tradition of writing responsa continues in contemporary times. A number of rabbis have even issued responsa on matters pertaining to modern technology. Consider the late Rabbi Moshe Feinstein, who wrote responsa on such topics as the permissibility of cosmetic surgery, how to make dishwashers kosher, and artificial insemination. No doubt the practice of issuing responsa will continue as Judaism continues to address increasingly complex issues, such as DNA cloning.

—— 19 ——

MIDRASHIM: INTERPRETIVE STORIES

Midrash is a method used to inquire into what a biblical text might mean. In Hebrew, the word *midrash* translates as "commentary" or "interpretation." It is based on a Hebrew root meaning "to investigate" or "to study."

You might suppose that after receiving and studying both the Written and Oral Torah, and then spending the first half of the first millennium promulgating the Talmud (the Mishna and Gemara), Judaism would have sufficient material to last the lifetime of even its most dedicated and erudite scholars. You'd think ample questions had been raised regarding Bible text, and enough dialogue and answers had developed. But of course, there is always more to study and learn.

Between the third and twelfth centuries, rabbis and religious scholars compiled their ideas and arguments into stories that probed even deeper into the underlying truths and meanings of biblical text. These stories, or *midrashim* (interpretations), became known as the Midrash.

In the Midrash, each interpretive story is designed to expand on incidents in the Bible, to derive principles and laws, or to offer moral lessons. Midrashim can be used to gain a glimpse into the thought processes of the rabbis who read and contemplated the biblical text.

Many midrashim deal with the story of Creation. For example, when God was ready to create man, He said, "Let us make man." But who is "us"? Wasn't God alone? The midrash explains this by concluding God was not alone and that God consulted with the angels.

As another example, let's look at a contemporary issue. Today, there is much controversy over the matter of capital punishment. But that issue is raised earlier, in the book of Genesis, through the story of Cain killing his brother Abel. While the Bible does allow for capital punishment, God does not inflict this penalty upon Cain. Why not?

The midrash addressing this question suggests that since Cain had never witnessed death, he could not possibly have known how his physical assault on Abel would culminate. Therefore, it would not have been just to take Cain's life—that's why he was sentenced to permanent exile instead.

The Midrash has become a major literary component of Judaism. The midrashim purport to penetrate the "spirit" of the material in question to reach a conclusion that is not necessarily obvious. There is no hesitancy to use poetic license, and rules of logic are not always relied upon.

20

Halakah: Jewish law and accumulated jurisprudence

Halakah is Jewish law and accumulated jurisprudence. The word *Halakah* means "law," but it may be translated literally as "the path that one walks." The word is derived from the Hebrew root of three letters, *heh-lamed-kaf*, which carries the meaning of travel or walking. From a practical standpoint, like all jurisprudence and legal rules, Halakah keeps things in check.

Judaism teaches that humans are dualistic creatures who have both a spiritual and a physical side. Thus, there is a constant tension and need to preserve a careful balance between those two sides. While the physical aspect is important, and the need to maintain a healthy body and satisfy corporeal pleasures is recognized, more importance is attached to the ethereal element of human nature, the soul. The physical body is the product of human parents. But the soul is the gift of God, and thus it should be the more cherished aspect of a human being.

Judaism acknowledges that, when left unchecked, human beings tend to be ruled by their own drives and desires, and they stray from acting in harmony with their spiritual side. Consequently, God gave the Jews the Halakah in order to keep the physical and spiritual aspects in balance.

The Halakah consists of *mitzvot* (commandments) from the Torah, laws enacted by rabbis, and established customs and traditions. For those who follow the Orthodox view, all are equally binding. However, the penalties provided for violating laws instituted by rabbis are less severe than those for violating the laws in the Torah.

It is probably impossible to comply with all of the commandments and laws. Many are inapplicable, and individuals are not expected to fulfill those things that don't apply to their situations.

It's important to note that the requirements of Halakah cannot be followed by rote, or they will lose their purpose. (It is this type of perfunctory behavior against which Hasidism rails.)

Unlike most codes of jurisprudence, Halakah does not consist only of prohibitions. Quite the contrary, there are instructions and obligations requiring the performance of affirmative actions. The various duties that Halakah imposes reflect the belief that they help to add a dimension of spirituality to human beings' lives.

Just as the *kohanim* (priests) in the Holy Temple diligently followed the requirements of Halakah that pertained to maintaining the sanctity of the Temple, Judaism likewise teaches that every Jewish home is, in its own way, a holy temple (*mikdash me'at*) that must be hallowed. This notion of holiness extends beyond the confines of the home: Each individual is also charged to do what he or she can to make the world more sacred.

This responsibility has been succinctly and repeatedly stated in the Torah: "So that you remember and do all My Commandments, and you will be holy to your God."

21

THE TEN STATEMENTS

When Moses led the Hebrews out of slavery in Egypt (see number 3), this was not the end of their journey to freedom. The Hebrews encountered more challenges before they reached Mount Sinai, where God gave Moses the 613 mitzvot, which Moses, in turn, gave to the people. Generally, mitzvot comprise all the laws and practices of Halakah, including those issued by the rabbis and established customs.

The first and foremost of all the mitzvot are the ten known in the Christian world as the Ten Commandments. This is a misnomer; the term "Ten Commandments" does not exist anywhere in the Torah. Although the word "commandments" appears in the King James Bible, it reflects an incorrect translation of the Hebrew. The words used in the Torah, *Aseret Had'varim*, may be better translated as "Ten Statements" or "Ten Words."

The Ten Statements appear twice in the Torah, at Exodus 20:2–14 and Deuteronomy 5:2–18. (There are a few minor discrepancies between the two.) The following list is taken from Exodus:

1. I am the Lord your God who brought you out of the land of Egypt, the house of bondage: You shall have no other gods beside Me.
2. You shall not make for yourself a sculptured image, or any likeness of what is in the heavens above, or on the earth below, or in the waters under the earth. You shall not bow down to them or

serve them. For I the Lord your God am an impassioned God, visiting the guilt of the fathers upon the children, upon the third and upon the fourth generations of those who reject Me, but showing kindness to the thousandth generation of those who love Me and keep My commandments.

3. You shall not swear falsely by the name of the Lord your God; for the Lord will not clear one who swears falsely by His name.

4. Remember the Sabbath day and keep it holy. Six days you shall labor and do all your work, but the seventh day is a Sabbath of the Lord your God: you shall not do any work—you, your son or daughter, your male or female slave, or your cattle, or the stranger who is within your settlements. For in six days the Lord made heaven and earth and sea, and all that is in them, and He rested on the seventh day; therefore, the Lord blessed the Sabbath day and hallowed it.

5. Honor your father and mother, that you may long endure on the land which the Lord your God is giving you.

6. You shall not murder.

7. You shall not commit adultery.

8. You shall not steal.

9. You shall not bear false witness against your neighbor.

10. You shall not covet your neighbor's house: you shall not covet your neighbor's wife, or his male or female slave, or his ox or his ass, or anything that is your neighbor's.

The Ten Statements are, indeed, commandments. However, as noted at the beginning of this point, they are part of 613 commandments in the Torah. As you will see in number 22, each of them fits into one of ten categories of commandments represented by the Ten Statements.

— 22 —

THE 613 MITZVOT

In its most limited sense, mitzvot are the commandments that appear in the Torah. The 613 mitzvot of the Torah are at the heart of the Halakah and deal with all aspects of our lives. However, the word *mitzvah* may be defined either as a "commandment" in general or as "divine commandment." It can also mean a "meritorious act" or "good deed." Many Jews who are not aware of this distinction frequently employ the second meaning. To them, mitzvah has come to mean doing a "good deed."

The number 613 is of consequence here because it is the numeric value of the word *Torah*. This is calculated as follows: tav = 400, vav = 6, resh = 200, heh = 5, plus 2 for the two mitzvot that precede the Torah text ("I am the Lord your God and you shall have no other gods before Me").

Because the 613 mitzvot emanate from God, these commandments cannot be changed or modified. They are, however, subject to interpretation, including the manner in which they are applied. Some of the mitzvot are obvious, while others are inferred, and yet others are ascertained by Talmudic logic. And while there are 613 distinct mitzvot, a number of these overlap or are repetitive.

Remember, what makes Halakah unique is that Jewish Law includes more than just prohibitions—it entails obligations as well. Hence, of the 613 mitzvot, 365 are negative and 248 are positive. The intention behind the act is critical. Rabbis have often used the phrase *simcha shel mitzva* to emphasize that a mitzvah performed out of a sense of requirement is not as meaningful as one performed out of desire and with enjoyment.

No person is capable of observing all 613 mitzvot. In fact, most do not apply to any given individual. Some of these mitzvot are pertinent only to the land of Israel. Others concern the Temple and *kohanim* (the priestly sect descended from Aaron), while many mitzvot deal with animal sacrifices and offerings.

Since it would be difficult to list all of the 613 mitzvot here in this book, perusing the following categories will help you to grasp the extent to which these commandments pervade the Jewish life. The mitzvot categories include commandments regarding the following:

- God
- Criminal laws
- Torah
- Punishment and restitution
- Signs and symbols
- Prophecy
- Prayer and blessings

- Idolatry and idolatrous practices
- Love and brotherhood
- Agriculture and animal husbandry
- The poor and unfortunate
- Clothing
- Marriage, divorce, and family
- The firstborn
- Sexual relations
- Kohanim and Levites (*Kohanim* are the priestly sect descended from Aaron; *Levites* are descendents of Levi, one of the sons of Jacob, whom God had charged with performing certain duties at the Temple.)
- Times and seasons
- Tithes and taxes
- Dietary laws
- The Temple and sacred objects
- Business practices
- Sacrifices and offerings
- Employees, servants, and slaves
- Ritual purity and impurity
- Vows, oaths, and swearing
- Lepers and leprosy
- Sabbatical and Jubilee years
- The King
- Court and judicial procedures

- Nazarites (In the Bible, these are men dedicated to God who, after taking a special vow, abstained from intoxicating beverages, never cut their hair, and so on. A Nazarite is a particularly dedicated and committed person.)
- Injuries and damages
- Wars
- Property and property rights

As you can see, some of the mitzvot categories are no longer applicable to modern life. Jews no longer need to concern themselves with laws associated with animal sacrifice, dealing with lepers, or keeping slaves, for instance. However, many subjects are still quite relevant, even though at first glance you may think otherwise.

23

OTHER LAWS: GEIZEIRAH, TAKKANAH, MINHAG, AND LASHON HA-RA

In addition to the commandments, rabbis assembled laws to help keep people from unintentionally violating a mitzvah. Any such law that is not a mitzvah but that still belongs to the Halakah is known as a *gezeirah*. In order to keep the mitzvah of avoiding work on the Sabbath, you would obey the gezeirah that instructs not to touch any implement of work.

A gezeirah also established the practice of adding a second day to the celebration of most holidays in the Diaspora. This way, Jews living outside Israel would not accidentally violate the command to celebrate the holiday because of some confusion with the calendar. Once uniform calendars became the norm, there was discussion of eliminating the added day, but the rabbis opted to continue the practice as a minhag—a custom that has been observed for so long and by so many that it has become binding.

Halakah also includes laws known as the *takkanah*. These laws are established by rabbis and may vary from one community to another. For example, since Hanukkah is a postbiblical holiday, the command to light candles during that time is a takkanah.

Although laws of gezeirah, takkanah, and minhag were incorporated into the Jewish tradition much later than the mitzvot of the Torah, they are now equally valid components of the Halakah.

There is yet another type of Jewish law, known as *lashon ha-ra*, which can be illustrated through a case that occurred in October 2001. Peter Levin, an attorney and legal pundit, found himself in a dilemma while he was covering the trial of Fred Neulander, a rabbi who stood accused of hiring a hit man to murder his wife. It seems word reached Mr. Levin from several rabbis that his reporting on the case might create a situation of lashon ha-ra (forbidden speech or slander). Having decided several years earlier to become a more observant Jew, Mr. Levin carefully reflected on his predicament but ultimately opted to report on the case.

What rabbis were concerned about specifically had to do with the laws proscribing gossip or utterances that wrong another. Judaism recognizes the harm that speech can cause. Unlike many other transgressions against another person, where restitution can often be made, hurtful words that leave a speaker's lips are like arrows shot from a bow. They cannot be retrieved, and their damage cannot be undone. Moreover, gossip and disparaging words may be inciting and result in violence.

Hence, there is no forgiveness for disparaging speech, and it is expressly prohibited. It is no matter whether what you say is true or false, whether it is a secret or known by others, or whether it is derogatory. While there are several exceptions to this ban, such as providing testimony in a court of law or revealing information to protect someone from serious harm, the bottom line is that it is forbidden to gossip.

— 24 —

Basic tenets: The Thirteen Principles of Faith

Exactly what Jews believe, or are expected to believe, is not precisely clear. Nor is there one accepted definition of Judaism acknowledged as absolute dogma. Part 1 includes an overview of the various branches of Judaism, which differ in their approaches to the faith. In spite of these differences, Judaism does encompass certain common tenets to which all religious Jews adhere. Maimonides, a twelfth-century influential Jewish thinker, outlined these tenets as the Thirteen Principles of Faith:

1. God exists.
2. God is one and unique.
3. God is incorporeal.
4. God is eternal.
5. Prayer is to be directed to God alone and to no other.
6. The words of the prophets are true.
7. Moses was the greatest of the prophets; his prophecies are true.
8. Moses received the Written Torah (first five books of the Bible) and the Oral Torah (teachings contained in the Talmud and other writings).
9. There will be no other Torah.
10. God knows the thoughts and deeds of men.
11. God will reward the good and punish the wicked.
12. The Messiah will come.
13. The dead will be resurrected.

Though brief, these tenets touch upon a range of serious theological issues. On what does Judaism rely to establish its basic tenets? How do you know what God wants you to do? Where did the Jews get the concept of the Messiah? The answers to these sorts of questions lie with the belief in the authenticity of the Torah, traditionally ascribed to Moses and the subsequent prophets.

Throughout the centuries, there were several additional attempts to create definitive codes, including the *Shulhan Arukh*, written by Rabbi Joseph Caro in the sixteenth century. Rabbi Joseph ben Ephraim Caro was born in Toledo, Spain, in 1488. Following the expulsion of the Jews from Spain, he wandered through Turkey, Bulgaria, and Greece, ultimately settling in Safed, Israel, where he died in 1575. (His gravestone is intact and a frequent stop for visitors to Safed.)

The *Shulhan Arukh* has its roots in Caro's earlier work, the *Beit Yosef* (House of Joseph), and it summarizes the conclusions reached in this prior text. In turn, the *Beit Yosef* was a detailed commentary of the *Tur*, by Rabbi Jacob ben Asher. The *Shulhan Arukh* is just one more example of how Jewish law evolved, and continues to do so today, by examining and building upon previous work and text.

Since the *Shulhan Arukh* was a summary, a number of rabbis initially opposed it, preferring the method of going back to the original sources. However, the *Shulhan Arukh* rapidly gained acceptance in almost all Jewish communities. Today, the *Shulhan Arukh* has come to be regarded as a defining criterion of religious Orthodoxy and traditionalism.

Although the degree to which the Jews take the Torah literally depends on the branch of Judaism they belong to (once again, refer to Part 1), the Torah is indeed Judaism's keystone.

Many Jews have devoted their entire lives to the study of Torah. Yet the essence of Judaism is splendid in its simplicity. Jews tell a story about Hillel, a great Jewish sage. As the story goes, a man once approached Hillel and asked him to explain the essence of Judaism while standing on one foot. To this, Hillel responded, "What is hurtful to you, do not do to others. That is the whole Torah; the rest is commentary. Now, go and study."

25

STRIVING TO COMPREHEND THE NATURE OF GOD

It is no small matter that seven of the Thirteen Principles of Faith (see previous point) set forth by Maimonides pertain to God. The Jews' relationship to God is fundamental to Judaism. The principal declaration of Jewish faith is the *Shema,* a prayer that begins with the following words: "Hear, O Israel: The Lord is our God, the Lord is one." This avowal affirms the belief in one God, a unity that encompasses everything.

Yet the Jews admit that comprehending God is beyond their ability. When Moses asked God for His name, he received the following enigmatic response: *"Ehyeh asher ehyeh"* (Exodus 3:14), which may be translated as "I am that I am," but literally means, "I will be what I will be," and has also been taken to mean "I am what I will be."

Despite these inherent complexities, Judaism does hold a number of concepts about the nature of God. Of course, the most important belief is that God is One. God is also considered to be the Creator of everything. Even many nonobservant Jews have held to this belief.

Baruch Spinoza, a Jewish philosopher who was excommunicated from the Jewish community for questioning the accepted nature of God, ultimately concluded that God "is the free cause of all things." Albert Einstein, a nonobservant Jew, compared the universe to a clock, with God as the clockmaker who cannot be envisaged or understood.

According to traditional Jewish belief, God is responsible for the creation of human beings, an unceasing process. A prominent piece of Jewish liturgy repeatedly describes God as *Avinu Malkeinu*, "Our Father, Our King." Judaism purports that we are all God's children.

While God is often described with anthropomorphic features, such portraits aren't literal. They are employed to help humans understand God's actions. The Jews know that God is incorporeal. He has no limbs, no parts; He is neither male nor female. God is referred to in the masculine simply because Hebrew has no gender-neutral nouns. Indeed, however, there are occasions when feminine terms are applied to God. For instance, the manifestation of God's presence that fills the universe is called *shechinah*, a feminine word.

Since God is incorporeal, Jews are forbidden to represent God in a physical form. (Such an act would be considered idolatry.) This admonition has been heeded in many ways, from the way Jews adorn synagogues to the prohibition of tattoos on the body. However, the prohibition to write the name of God has nothing to do with this commandment, or with the commandment that prohibits Jews from taking the Lord's name in vain. The fact is, Jews may not write down God's name because they are enjoined from erasing or defacing it. Because no one can ever be certain what may subsequently happen to the paper (or any other medium) written with God's name, avoiding writing it down in the first place ensures that it cannot be destroyed. The source for this practice is found in Deuteronomy 12:3, which recounts how God commands the Hebrews to obliterate the names of all local deities, but not the name of God, when they take over the Promised Land.

Judaism holds that God is omnipotent (all-powerful), omniscient (all-knowing), and omnipresent (filling all places at all times). God is eternal. Past and future, here and now, are irrelevant in terms of God. Einstein attempted to describe this idea in more scientific terms: For God, "a thousand years and a thousand dimensions are as one."

Now, you may ask, if God is eternal and did act in history and intervene in human affairs in the past, why doesn't God continue to do so now? Where has God been hiding? An important principle of Judaism does offer an explanation grounded in the notion that the relationship between God and people is reciprocal. One way this has been expressed is in the following Hasidic tale:

> "Where is the dwelling of God?" This was the question with which the rabbi of Kotzk surprised a number of learned men who happened to be visiting him. They laughed at him: "What a thing to ask! Is not the whole world full of his glory?" Then he answered his own question. "God dwells wherever man lets him in."

Martin Buber, the twentieth-century Jewish philosopher and scholar, used the phrase "eclipse of God" as a metaphor to demonstrate something that has come between people and God, a something that may well be within ourselves. Imagine you are standing under a bright, glaring sun. You raise your hand and lift your thumb so it blocks the sun from sight. The sun is no longer visible. You cannot see it. Yet, it is there just the same. All you have to do to experience its existence is to remove your thumb.

So it is with God. Before experiencing God, you must first remove the impediment you have erected.

--- 26 ---

THE ETERNAL NATURE OF THE SOUL

The idea of a soul (*neshamah* in Hebrew) is fundamental to Judaism, which sees the soul as eternal. Although clear references to the human soul do appear in the Bible, most of what the Jewish tradition teaches about the soul comes from rabbinical (postbiblical) times. The soul comes from God, and it precedes the existence of a human body. As for where the soul is headed after this life, we are told in Ecclesiastes that the soul returns to God (thus, the idea of an afterlife): "The dust returns to the earth as it was, and the spirit returns to God who gave it" (12:7).

In Judaism, the soul is not indivisible. Rather, it is more like an amalgamation of five basic elements that are, in turn, subdivided into even more elements. This complicated subject has a lot to do with *Kabbalah* (Jewish mysticism). Though only briefly touched upon here, you will learn more about Kabbalah in number 31.

The lowest constituent of the soul is *nefesh*, and it is the soul's most physical aspect. In ascending order, the soul's other, more spiritual elements are *ruach*, *neshamah*, *chayah*, and *yechidah*. To refer to all five of these components, you can use the term *narachai* (an acronym of the five terms). Since the naranchai is numinous, it seeks spirituality, which is why humans seek to pursue the spiritual.

After a person dies, that person's naranchai will desire to leave the physical body. If the person has led a spiritual life, this desire will be fulfilled. However, the naranchai of those who were focused on the material aspect of the world may remain rooted to the physical. It gets more complex, but the point is there is a soul within each of us. To what extent it reaches its spiritual destination depends upon how we live our lives.

— 27 —

THE JEWISH CONCEPT OF THE AFTERLIFE

What is beyond the world as we know it, and where will the soul of a dead person dwell? Although Judaism focuses primarily on life in the here-and-now, the belief in an afterlife is well established in the Torah. In several places, there are indications that the righteous, but not the wicked, will be reunited with their loved ones. A number of biblical luminaries (Abraham, Jacob, Moses, and others) are said to have been "gathered to their people" after their death.

While the idea of an afterlife is firmly established in traditional Judaism, little in the way of doctrine and tenets surrounds it. As a result, you will find different concepts of the afterlife within Judaism, including some that consider the entire notion irrelevant.

Some Orthodox are of the opinion that wicked souls will be tormented by demons of their own making or they will cease to exist. There are those, such as many Hasidic sects, who believe in reincarnation—an element in Kabbalah. Some hold that the souls of the righteous are reborn to continue their good work, while other sources indicate that a soul is reincarnated only if there's a need to complete some unfinished business. Still others think life after death is a matter of waiting for resurrection.

Reincarnation and resurrection are not incompatible, and one does not preclude the other. Regardless of what ideas a person chooses to accept or reject about the soul and the afterlife, a Jew is still expected to live his or her life in accordance with the Jewish laws and principles.

During biblical times, the Jews believed in *sheol*, a world of shadows wherein dwell the dead. Later, they came to believe in a paradise called *Gan Eden* (Garden of Eden), not to be confused with the famous garden inhabited by Adam and Eve. This concept is somewhat similar to the Christian idea of Heaven.

Only the righteous will go directly to Gan Eden. Most souls descend to *Gehinnom*, the valley of Hinnom, which is a place of punishment or purification. (Conceptually, this notion of Gehinnom has some similarity to, and may have exerted influence on, the development of the idea of purgatory in the Roman Catholic tradition.) Gehinnom is named for a place that really existed in biblical times. Located outside Jerusalem, the historical Gehinnom was inhabited by pagans who offered their children as sacrifices, thus earning a reputation as the most abominable place imaginable.

Souls are not consigned to Gehinnom for eternity but only for a limited time. The idea of a soul being damned forever is not consistent with Judaism. In fact, the Jewish tradition maintains that all souls will ultimately be resurrected.

28

RESURRECTION AND THE WORLD TO COME

Although traditional Judaism does hold that all souls will be resurrected, there is no complete agreement on the details—an account that follows is only one scenario. The notion of resurrection has never been universally accepted in Judaism. Initially, the Pharisees (the forerunners of Rabbinical Judaism) deduced the concept from the Torah, but the Sadducees rejected the idea because it was not explicitly mentioned. Nonetheless, the belief in resurrection and afterlife is fundamental in traditional Judaism.

All ideas regarding resurrection have one point in common: Resurrection cannot take place until the coming of the Messiah, who will usher in the Messianic Era. Actually, in Judaism, it is believed there will be a succession of three messiahs. The word *messiah* means "anointed" and, therefore, does not rule out more than one messiah. The first messiah will be the first king who governs over a world that, while still physical, will be a wonderful place in which to live. People will still die, but they will lead long and healthy lives. Some believe that the righteous dead will be resurrected at this time to experience this perfect world. After the death of the first messiah, his son, and then grandson, will succeed him. Since the Messianic Era spans 2,000 years, these messiahs will live a very long time!

At the conclusion of the Messianic Era, the world as we know it, *Olam Ha-Zeh* ("this world"), will come to an end. A 1,000-year interval known as the years of desolation will follow. Nothing will be alive and all souls will be in the Realm of Souls engaged in a state of spiritual growth while awaiting the World to Come.

When the World to Come, or *Olam Ha-Ba*, arrives, each soul will be reunited with its body (that is, each human being will be resurrected), and humans will live in the World to Come for eternity. The Talmud and Midrash provide much of what we know of Olam Ha-Ba.

Although some have suggested that the wicked will not have a share in the World to Come, it is more widely held that all souls will be gathered together there. However, any particular soul's place, or its share in Olam Ha-Ba, is largely based on how it lived and the mitzvot it performed as a human being.

Do not confuse the World to Come with the Messianic Era. Although sometimes the two terms are used interchangeably, this is incorrect. The Messianic Era that accompanies the Messiah's appearance takes place in This World, which precedes the World to Come.

Does Judaism have a timetable for when the Messianic Era and the World to Come will finally arrive? Yes, but like most schedules, it doesn't always quite work out. The original plan was for the world to last 6,000 years, including 2,000 years of void before Abraham. The Messiah was slated to appear 2,000 years after Abraham and then there would be the 2,000 years of the Messianic Age. However, people have failed to adequately pave the way for the coming of the Messiah, so things are a bit off schedule. Today, we are well beyond the 2,000-year interval between Abraham and the Messiah.

While we cannot be certain when the Messiah will arrive and set things in motion for the World to Come, we can be sure about one thing—that all of us will die in This World (Olam Ha-Zeh).

All humans will enter the Olam Ha-Ba. Furthermore, because one's position in Olam Ha-Ba is predicated upon righteousness and not just belief, the religion that any human being professed or followed during life on earth is irrelevant. All the righteous, regardless of their religious beliefs or cultural backgrounds, share the World to Come.

For more on how Judaism treats death, read the following point, as well as the last three sections of Part 5.

29

HONORING THE DEAD

As explained in number 28, the souls of the dead eventually end up in Olam Ha-Ba, where they will be reunited with their bodies, emerging as ultimately spiritual beings. In Judaism, the body is an indispensable part of that new, ethereal being.

In general, Jewish burial customs derive from the concept of *Kevod Ha-Met* ("honor due to the dead"). The same concept also provides the Jews with explicit guidelines for how to behave toward the deceased's body, which is treated with the utmost respect.

Once a person dies, someone must close the body's eyes and mouth, cover its face, and light candles. It is customary to lay the body with feet pointing toward the door; the body may be laid on the floor.

From the moment of death until the deceased is buried, known as the *aninut* period, the mourner's chief responsibility is to attend to the deceased and make the necessary funeral and burial preparations. Because these tasks take priority, mourners are exempt from all positive, time-honored mitzvot. Judaism requires a prompt interment, and so aninut lasts a day or two. During this time, it is inappropriate to make condolence calls.

Out of respect for the deceased, the dead body is never left alone from the moment of death until burial. Sometimes arrangements are made for someone to sit with the body. These sentinels are called *shomerim* (from the root *shin-mem-resh* that means "guards" or "keepers"). The shomerim recite Psalms and may not eat, drink, or perform mitzvot in the presence of the deceased because performing a commandment of God is a joyous action.

Because the Torah forbids leaving a body unburied overnight (Deuteronomy 21:23), the burial process happens rather quickly (though in present times the internment actually occurs one or two days after death). This haste to the cemetery, has to do with reverence for the dead body, not a desire to get rid of it and move on.

If there is a local burial society, often known as *Chevra Kadisha* ("the holy society"), the relatives contact its representative in order that they may prepare the body. The alternative is for a Jewish funeral home to assume the responsibilities regarding the body. The deceased must be cleaned and wrapped in a simple shroud (*tashrichim*), usually made of white linen. The reason for the uniformity in attiring the deceased is that all people are alike, wealthy and poor, and nothing should distinguish one from the other at death. This is also one of the reasons each person is buried in a plain wooden coffin.

However, many Jewish families deviate from some of these procedures. For example, the body may be dressed in clothes and not a shroud, and the coffin may be made of a material more durable than wood. Though cremation and entombment are prohibited, some Jews nevertheless opt for these alternatives.

Jewish tradition discourages autopsies and organ transplants out of respect for the body. However, where required by law or to save a life, these prohibitions may be ignored. Traditionally, Jewish corpses do not undergo embalming or cosmetology, although, once again, it is not unusual for many Jewish families to select these procedures.

Jewish keepers should not forget to open a window in the room where the deceased is at rest. While not always followed, this custom has to do with the belief that the window should be open so the neshamah (soul) can escape as soon as possible.

─── 30 ───

Spirituality and mysticism: Connecting to divine sparks

What is life all about? Is there any meaning to it? Who am I? Will there be an afterlife, or is this all there is to human existence? Is there such a thing as a soul? These sorts of existential questions plague most everyone at one time or another. Maybe you pondered many of these conundrums when you were an adolescent or in college, and perhaps they still vex you, even now.

Many people turn to various religions to find answers to these puzzles. Although Judaism places emphasis on laws and codes of behavior, it also has a spiritual component that runs deep and dates to its beginnings. (Although spirituality and mysticism have a distinct place in Judaism, be aware that not all Jews recognize this to be the case. In fact, most Ashkenazic Jews either refrain from acknowledging this mystical component or minimize its significance.)

Jewish spirituality actually originates with Abraham, who is said to be the first Kabbalist. The Torah contains numerous stories about angels, prophetic dreams and visions, and other mystical experiences. The Talmud (the collection of oral interpretations of the Torah) does not flinch from addressing the question of the soul, and it suggests that a mystical school of thought was taught to advanced students. Later still, many mystical teachings were set down in books like the Zohar.

No matter what variation of Jewish spirituality, the religion is grounded in the basic doctrines of Judaism, holding fast to a belief in one God who is the Creator of all things. Since God created the world, according to the Jewish tradition, holiness is to be found by encountering the world, not withdrawing from it.

If Judaism's spirituality and mysticism had to be summed up in one word, that word would be "sparks." But what, exactly, does that mean? It all has to do with the way spiritual Judaism views Creation.

In the Jewish tradition, it is said that divine energy poured into the void, creating a seamless vessel of supernal light. But this God-energy was so intense that it shattered the vessel it was shaping, causing it to explode into a multitude of sparks. These sparks of holy light dispersed. Because they were disconnected from each other and in a state of alienation, each spark became obscured by a shell of darkness. You can find a darkened spark of holiness in exile at the root of every soul, in each and every thing and act, and in every relationship.

The entire purpose of Jewish mysticism, whether Kabbalistic or Hasidic, is to gather these sparks and to bring them back into a holy whole. (See numbers 14 and 15 for more on Hasidic Judaism.) Obviously, this is not something people can do in seclusion. Hence, Jewish spirituality requires that people go out into the world, engaging with it in a concerted effort to release holy sparks from imprisonment, gathering these sparks so they are free to return to the divine light. At such a time, the world can become one in God and will have been redeemed.

The divine sparks are in all things, including humans. From the mystical viewpoint, a divine spark is what you might otherwise call the soul, but it lies dormant within a person, encased by the body surrounding it.

This soul, or transcendent self, has a burning desire to attach itself to God, but in order to begin this voyage, a person's soul must become receptive and allow the surrounding light to enter.

How does a person receive this light, and where is it to be found? It is found in this world. Spiritual Judaism teaches Jews how to open themselves up and absorb the world—in other words, how to receive the light. Even the mystical aspect of Judaism emphasizes the reciprocal nature of the relationship between humans and God. Unlike most other forms of spirituality and mysticism, Judaism's unique interpretation stresses contact with the world. It is only through direct interaction with and involvement in the world that God can be experienced. This mystical school of thought in Judaism is what has come to be known as Kabbalah.

31

THE KABBALAH

The word *Kabbalah* comes from the Hebrew verb *lekabbel*, which means "to receive" or "to accept." Kabbalah teaches people how to empower themselves to reach the spiritual world by enhancing their "sixth sense." This sixth sense is also called the spiritual vessel (*kli*), and is independent of material reality. Ordinarily, kli is not sufficiently developed to make contact with the spiritual world. By studying Kabbalah, however, a person's soul can widen, allowing the surrounding light to enter it.

Kabbalah is like a mathematics of emotions. It takes the total of all feelings and desires, divides them, and then provides an exact mathematical formula for each and every circumstance. Kabbalah combines emotions and intellect, infusing an element of spirituality to study.

It is said Kabbalistic knowledge was passed down from Abraham and through the generations. As with Halakah, Kabbalah evolved by word of mouth, with each Kabbalist leaving his own unique imprint.

Preserving this knowledge became pressing after the destruction of the Second Temple in 70 C.E. Following the failed revolt of Bar Kochba and the execution of Rabbi Akiva (a key figure of the rabbinic period and a master of Halakah) in the second century, Rabbi Shimon Bar Yochai (also known by the abbreviation Rashbi) escaped with his son and went into seclusion for thirteen years. Emerging from the cave in which he had hidden, the Rashbi brought forth the Zohar, the preeminent Kabbalistic writing that provided a method of achieving spirituality.

But the Rashbi did not actually write the Zohar. He worked it out in his head and later dictated his thoughts to Rabbi Aba, who transcribed the material in the form of parables, in Aramaic.

The Zohar teaches that human development progresses over 6,000 years. During this period, souls undergo a continuous process of growth, at the end of which all souls reach the highest level of spirituality and wholeness.

Eventually, the Zohar mysteriously vanished, only to reappear again centuries later among secret groups of Kabbalists who studied it as a holy text. In the sixteenth century, Rabbi Yitzhak Luria, known as the Ari, provided a basic system for studying Kabbalah. He also produced writings that, for the first time, presented the pure language of Kabbalah.

In the sixteenth and seventeenth centuries, small groups of Kabbalistic scholars continued to study the Zohar. Then, from the mid-eighteenth century until the beginning of the twentieth century (known as the great Hassidut period), the Zohar assumed a prominent position in Judaism. In fact, many prominent rabbis were involved in Kabbalism during that time.

As the twentieth century progressed, interest in the Kabbalah waned until it practically disappeared. Although at present, the study of Kabbalah is once again gaining in popularity and there are Kabbalah centers throughout the United States, Kabbalah remains an alien and esoteric subject for the majority of Jews.

If you are interested in Kabbalah, you may not want to study it until you are well versed in Torah. In the past, Kabbalah was not taught to anyone under the age of forty because it was believed that a comprehensive understanding of Judaism was first necessary. There was also a concern that receiving instruction in Kabbalah could prove harmful to the mental and emotional health of a young person, because this powerful and advanced form of study can be overwhelming.

— 32 —

UNDERSTANDING GOD'S ESSENCE THROUGH
THE KABBALISTIC TREE OF LIFE

Kabbalah is a mysterious and complicated system of ideas. It is not easily accessible to all and is certainly beyond the scope of this book to explain it in its entirety. Just to give you an introductory sense of the Kabbalah, however, this section will take a look at one of its more fundamental and better-known concepts, the Tree of Life.

In Judaism, God is believed to exist beyond time and space. Consequently, Kabbalah asks the question, "How can there be any interaction between God and humans, who are limited by the context of time and space?" The answer lies in the Tree of the Sefirot, also called the Kabbalistic Tree of Life.

According to Kabbalistic tradition, since the true essence of God, *Ein Sof* (without end), is so transcendent that it cannot have any interchange with the universe, contact is achieved by way of the ten emanations from God's essence, known as the Ten Sefirot. These Ten Sefirot correspond to the qualities of God. They are:

1. Keter (the crown)
2. Chokhmah (wisdom)
3. Binah (intuition, understanding)
4. Chesed (mercy) or Gedulah (greatness)

5. Gevurah (strength)
6. Tiferet (glory)
7. Netzach (victory)
8. Hod (majesty)
9. Yesod (foundation)
10. Malkut (sovereignty)

The Ten Sefirot are generally represented in a diagram that resembles a tree, which is why the schema is commonly referred to as the Tree of the Sefirot or the Kabbalistic Tree of Life. These Sefirot are part of God, and yet they are capable of interacting with the universe, including human beings. The Sefirot experience the good and evil human deeds, which thus affect the entire universe and God.

— 33 —

ESTABLISHING JUSTICE THROUGH GOOD DEEDS

If you recall, 248 out of 613 mitzvot involve positive action. That's what *tzedakah* (charity) is all about, the performing of good deeds. To be specific, "charity" is actually a misnomer; in fact, there is no Hebrew word for charity. *Tzedakah* comes from the root *tzedek* (righteous). The idea behind tzedakah involves the obligation to establish justice by being righteous, compassionate, and helpful to others.

In Judaism, practicing tzedakah is an obligation. The twelfth-century Jewish thinker Maimonides organized the fulfilling of tzedakah into various degrees of giving, beginning with the least meritorious:

- Giving begrudgingly
- Giving less than you should, but giving it cheerfully
- Giving after being asked
- Giving before being asked
- Giving when you do not know the recipient's identity, but the recipient knows your identity
- Giving when you know the recipient's identity, but the recipient does not know your identity
- Giving when neither party knows the other's identity
- Enabling the recipient to become self-reliant

Jewish families and congregations will sometimes set up a tzedakah, or *pushke*, in homes or synagogues as a repository for charity money they collect. The strength of mutual support in the Jewish tradition is one of the characteristics that embraces those who are not religiously observant.

— 34 —

THE JEWISH OUTLOOK ON
INTERFAITH MARRIAGE AND DIVORCE

In traditional Judaism, a marriage between Jew and Gentile is not an issue or open to question. It is forbidden, and that's that. Some reasons are spiritual, such as the notion that a Jewish marriage reunites two parts of the same soul. How can it be possible for one of the halves to be non-Jewish?

This prohibition also stems from more practical considerations. For one thing, there is the matter of the viability of the Jewish people. It would be difficult to remain a distinct religious and ethnic group if intermarriage was widespread. In the United States, where the intermarriage rate is 50 percent, only a quarter of children born in these marriages are raised as Jews. The Jewish population in the United States is actually decreasing.

Nonetheless, interfaith marriages have existed all through history and cannot be ignored. Although the Reform and Reconstructionist branches of Judaism do not encourage intermarriages, they have adopted a more accepting approach. If the non-Jewish bride or groom chooses not to convert, there is always the option of having a joint-faith ceremony with clergy members of both faiths present. However, under these circumstances, it is more difficult to secure the services of a rabbi.

Bear in mind that the conversion process selected determines the type of rabbi who will officiate and what branch of Judaism will recognize the marriage. The Orthodox will acknowledge a marriage and an

Orthodox rabbi will officiate at the ceremony only if the conversion was consistent with Orthodox requirements.

Judaism is pragmatic about marriage and has always been realistic about the fact that some marriages may end in divorce. The Jewish marriage contract (the *ketubah*; see number 80 for more information) makes provisions for what happens in the event of divorce. However, while the ketubah is designed to protect the woman, the rules of divorce are definitely lopsided in favor of the man.

Under Jewish law, a woman cannot commence divorce proceedings, yet a man can divorce his wife for any reason or no reason at all. (Though if the husband is unable to provide a rational reason, the rabbi will suggest counseling or reconsideration.) There are also cases in which a man must divorce his wife, regardless of whether he wants to, for example, if she has committed adultery. Though it may seem easy for a man to secure a divorce, the truth is that the process is far from simple.

In the Torah, a divorce is accomplished by writing a bill of divorce called a *sefer k'ritut* (scroll of cutting off), delivering it to the wife, and sending her away. In fact, the Hebrew word for divorce is *gerushin*, a term that comes from the Hebrew verb "to send away." Today, the Jewish divorce is known as a *get*, a "bill of divorce" in Hebrew.

The procedures involved in obtaining a get are complicated. Although the woman must be provided for financially, once again, the laws generally favor the husband. However, over the years, efforts have been made to bring greater equality into the process. For example, while only a man can initiate a divorce, it is now necessary for the wife to agree to it.

Judaism's particular attitude to divorce has led to another problem. If a man deserts his wife or disappears and no proof of his death exists, his wife technically remains married—since a woman cannot initiate a divorce. A woman in such a situation is referred to as *agunah* (anchored). She cannot remarry because, in the event her husband is alive, the rabbis do not want to have condoned an adulterous marriage.

In order to be divorced after having been married according to the laws and customs of Judaism, the Orthodox and Conservative movements require that a get be obtained. Reform and Reconstructionist Judaism, on the other hand, generally recognize a civil decree.

— 35 —

WHAT DOES KEEPING KOSHER MEAN?

Kashrut are dietary laws that specifically set forth the foods Jews are permitted to eat and how these foods must be prepared. The word *kashrut* means "fit," "proper," or "appropriate." Adhering to the laws of kashrut calls for greater attention and respect of food, and maintaining a kosher kitchen ensures that a home remains open to observant Jews.

In times past, eating and drinking carried grave religious obligations. Strict adherence to dietary laws reinforced the Jews' identity as being a holy and chosen people. Further, some have claimed that the Jewish dietary laws afforded beneficial health effects, although this became less of a factor with the advent of refrigeration.

The primary reason for keeping kosher is because God commanded their fulfillment as mitzvot. In fact, the laws of kashrut belong to a category of mitzvot known as *chukkim,* laws that don't have any logical reasons behind them. Although certain branches of Judaism do not require members to adhere to kashrut, and others are less demanding in its application, keeping kosher is a fundamental component of Halakah.

Treyf is any food or thing that is not kosher. This may include foods that are prohibited for consumption in general as well as foods prepared incorrectly. The Torah specifies animals that do not have cloven hooves and do not chew their cud may not be eaten—hence, no pork. As for seafood, observant Jews are restricted to fish that have both fins and scales—so shellfish are forbidden. Products derived from treyf animals are likewise not permitted—this applies to milk, eggs, fat, and organs.

Although Judaism does not require vegetarianism, the method in which animals are slaughtered and primed is critical. Animals may be slain for food, skins, and clothing only when there is a genuine need. Cruelty toward animals and hunting for sport are strictly forbidden.

Animals must be slaughtered in the most humane way possible, and there are specific mitzvot that govern animal slaughter. The ritual slaughterer, known as a *shochet,* carries out this act with a swift stroke of the blade across the animal's throat. Animals who have not been slaughtered properly are deemed treyf and may not be consumed.

According to the Torah, the essence of life is in the blood. To consume the blood of an animal is to consume its life—an act strictly prohibited.

Consequently, following slaughter, animals must be drained of blood. All residual blood is drained from the meat during food preparation, either by broiling, soaking, or salting.

Probably one of the better-known aspects of kashrut is the separation of meat and dairy products. The basis for this is found in the Torah: "You shall not boil a kid in its mother's milk," a statement that appears in the Torah three times.

The separation includes not only the foods themselves but also the utensils involved in cooking, the plates and flatware used to serve and eat the food, and the towels and dishwashers employed in cleaning up. Further, Jews who observe these dietary laws must wait at least several hours before moving from *fleishig* (meat) to *milchig* (dairy) to avoid mixing inside their own bodies!

Often, restaurants and food markets may advertise kosher-style products, but such products are not necessarily kosher. Traditional Jewish foods such as bagels, blintzes, and even *matzah* (unleavened bread eaten at Passover) and grape wine may not be kosher if they are not prepared in strict accordance with kashrut.

Part 3

RELIGIOUS SERVICES
AND OBJECTS

PRAYERS ARE AN IMPORTANT PART OF JUDAISM. THEY range from daily private prayers, blessings, and recitations, to public prayers that are part of the liturgy recited in the synagogue. This section will explore the special place that prayer occupies in Judaism, as well as where and how Jews pray.

Because Judaism accepts both public and private prayer, there is no need for guidance or help in worshipping. However, traditional roles for synagogue functionaries have gradually evolved. To understand how synagogue services work, it will be helpful for you to learn more about these roles and the objects and practices related to prayer and religious services. Many Jewish objects and symbols were created in order to observe mitzvot, while others are derived from custom and tradition.

— 36 —

WHAT IT MEANS TO BE A RABBI

A rabbi is not a priest. Nor is a rabbi an intermediary between a person and God. A rabbi has no more authority to discharge Jewish rituals than any other Jew. It isn't even necessary for a rabbi to lead prayer services—anyone can do this. As a result, there is a true democratic form of worship in Jewish services.

The precursors to those who officiate at Jewish religious services are the *kohanim* (or *kohein* in the singular), descendants of Aaron who were enjoined by God to perform certain sacred duties in connection with the services in the Temple. The services, described in detail in the Torah, had to do with animal sacrifices and purity ceremonies. However, the role of this priestly class became largely irrelevant after the Temple's destruction. Today, a rabbi need not be a kohein, since his position has nothing whatsoever to do with the tasks performed by the priests in the days of the Temple.

The Levites, from the tribe of Levi, were another caste of Jews with special responsibilities related to Temple service. However, their duties were less illustrious than those of the kohanim. Naturally, their jobs also ceased to exist after the Temple was destroyed.

For centuries, there has been very little to distinguish the kohanim from the Levites. However, some distinctions remain in religious practices. For example, the first *aliyah* (recital of a blessing over the Torah reading) is given to a kohein on Shabbat. The second aliyah is assigned to a Levite. This reflects the kohanim's special status as the priestly class.

What, then, *does* it mean to be a rabbi? The most significant clue can be found in the meaning of the word itself. The word *rabbi* comes to us from the Hebrew word *rabi*, which means "my teacher." Once the Temple laid in ruins and Jews were scattered all over the globe, the thing that probably held the Jews together was their knowledge of Torah. Learning became the highest priority, and rabbis (teachers) became community leaders.

How does someone become a rabbi? The answer is much different today than it was thousands of years ago. According to tradition, Joshua became a rabbi when Moses laid his hands on Joshua's head and "ordained" him. The Hebrew term for ordination is *semicha* (to lean upon). Originally, in order to become a rabbi, a man had to study with a rabbi who had been ordained through the semicha process. Once the studies were completed, the semicha procedure would be consummated with the setting of hands upon the head. Through this tradition, all rabbis had a direct link to Moses.

The process of semicha had largely come to an end by the year 200 C.E., after the destruction of the Second Temple in 70 C.E. and the subsequent dispersion of the Jewish people. In the centuries that followed, there was no set formula for becoming a rabbi. Instead, rabbis generally attained their status by studying Halakah and tradition. A rabbi had to be able to answer questions that were posed by members of the community.

Today, although a rabbi remains a respected figure in Judaism, his authority is derived from his position as a person of knowledge and not out of any special relationship to God. When a rabbi leads a prayer service—as rabbis generally do—they are at the forefront because this is a place they earned through hard work and study, not because of hierarchical status.

At present, a person becomes a rabbi by attending a yeshiva or seminary. After graduation, the rabbi is ordained, usually through one of the branches of Judaism. It is still possible to become a rabbi by being ordained by another rabbi, though this is rarely performed. In Israel, it is not uncommon to be ordained by both the Chief Rabbinate and an individual rabbi. (The latter practice is called a "private" semicha.)

—— *37* ——

WHAT DOES A CANTOR DO?

In Judaism, most prayers are frequently chanted (sung). Often, singing prayers during services is a job designated for a person other than the rabbi—the cantor.

The cantor (*chazzen*) leads the congregation in prayer chanting. Generally, the cantor sings the opening words of a prayer, the congregation joins in, and then the cantor sings the final verse. The cantor plays a pivotal role in the service because his melodies should inspire and assist the congregants in mustering *kavanah* (intent, or the proper state of spiritual concentration) for prayer.

Nothing in Judaism obligates a congregation to have a cantor, nor are specific qualifications required for the position. Typically, any person with good moral character, an ability to sing, and a knowledge of the prayers and tunes can serve as a chazzen.

In modern times, cantors are trained professionals. They may have been ordained as clergy, or they may have earned university degrees and/or teaching certificates. Some Reform, Conservative, and Reconstructionist synagogues have opened the post of the cantor to women as well.

Aside from leading the congregation in the prayers, the cantor may prepare young people to chant the *Haftorah* (weekly Torah portion) for their bar or bat mitzvah. While the cantor's status as religious leader and educator has become prominent in most synagogues, some smaller congregations cannot afford to hire a full- or even part-time professional. Sometimes a cantorial student is hired, but if this is not feasible, then either the rabbi or a *gabbai* (lay person who volunteers to fulfill duties in the religious service) assumes the responsibility.

— 38 —

THE IMPORTANCE OF PRAYER

The Hebrew word for "prayer" is *tefilah*. This word is derived from the verb *lehitpalel* (to judge oneself), which reflects the introspective aspect of prayer. Eastern European Jews also use the word *daven* (pray), which is derived from the English word "divine"; this word choice indicates that prayer is directed toward God.

The Talmud defines prayer as *avodat halev*, the "service of the heart," because prayer should express the deepest feelings and longing of the soul. More observant Jews use the entire body when praying. This practice is known as *shuckling* (swaying).

In Judaism, prayer is more than a matter of self-assessment that you can accomplish by setting aside some quiet time to contemplate, taking a solitary walk in the woods, or as many people have done, engaging in meditation (practiced particularly by those engaged in Judaism's mystical element). Judaism expects more than just reflection. It demands that the praying person involve the whole of his or her being in prayer.

The word that best describes the nature of Jewish prayer is *kavanah* (intent). Prayer is to be neither taken for granted nor performed perfunctorily. Words should not be recited by rote. What you say when praying is not as important as how you say it.

Consider this Hasidic tale that illustrates kavanah better than any scholarly elucidation. On the day after Yom Kippur, the Ba'al Shem Tov ordered his driver to take him to an inn in the forest. As soon as he entered, the owner begged to confess to the Ba'al Shem Tov how on Yom Kippur, while having every intention to go to *shul* (synagogue), he simply could not get away from his establishment since one customer after another continued to arrive. When he realized that it was too late to go to services, he decided to pray by himself. Not having learned Hebrew, all the poor innkeeper could do was recite the Hebrew alphabet and after doing this, he added, "Here, God, here are your holy letters, you put them into the right words. . . ."

The Ba'al Shem Tov put his arms around the man and said, "It was revealed to me in a vision that on this Yom Kippur your prayers had opened the gates of heaven, and I came to find out how to do it."

While the innkeeper was ignorant of the Yom Kippur liturgy and was not proficient in Hebrew, the Ba'al Shem Tov instantly saw how special the innkeeper's prayers had been because the man was filled with kavanah. What mattered was his intention—without kavanah, reciting all the prayers in the *Siddur* (prayer book) would be pointless.

Without doubt, the oldest daily prayer in Judaism is the *Shema*. The Shema is recited in the morning and at night, as commanded in its first paragraph, "When you recline [retire] and when you arise." Soon after the Babylonian Exile, Judaism saw the introduction of another central prayer, the *Shemoneh Esrei* (translated as eighteen prayers), a multifaceted prayer comprised of nineteen benedictions (eighteen original ones plus an additional benediction that was added later on).

Jewish Prayers

For more information on the Shema and other Jewish prayers, refer to Judaism 101, an online encyclopedia of all things Jewish that details beliefs, customs, prayers, scripture, and more, at *www.jewfaq.org/prayref.htm*.

The most important thing to remember about prayer in Judaism is that a Jew can pray anywhere. This is beautifully expressed in *Midrash Tehillim*: "When you pray, pray in the synagogue of your city; if you are unable to pray in the synagogue, pray in your field; if you are unable to pray in your field, pray in your home; if you are unable to pray in your home, pray on your couch; and if you are unable to pray on your couch, meditate in your heart."

—— 39 ——

HOUSE OF PRAYER: THE SYNAGOGUE

Although Jews can pray anywhere, Judaism prefers that prayer be conducted in an assemblage. Special places dedicated for prayer are generally called synagogues. The word *synagogue* is a Greek translation of the Hebrew *beit k'nesset* (place of assembly), and related to English word *synod*.

The origin of the synagogue is not clear. There are those who believe synagogues were in place during the time of the First Temple, while others maintain synagogues grew out of devotional services that accompanied the daily sacrifices in the Second Temple. Some also hold the opinion that the synagogue is a product of Jews in exile in Greek-influenced lands.

However, most scholars trace the synagogue's beginnings to the Babylonian Exile in the sixth century B.C.E. By the time the Second Temple fell (70 C.E.), there seems to have been a synagogue present wherever Jews dwelt throughout the Roman world. It is estimated that as many as 480 synagogues were in existence in Jerusalem around that time.

A synagogue can serve several purposes. It is best known as *beit hatefillah*, a house of prayer. Since Jews are encouraged to pray in groups and certain prayers require the presence of a *minyan* (ten adults), there must be a physical facility to accommodate the gathering.

In modern times, several different terms are used to denote the Jewish house of prayer. While the Conservative movement usually uses the word *synagogue*, Reform Jews often employ the word *temple*, referring to the Temple in Jerusalem. The Ashkenazic Orthodox commonly use *shul*, a Yiddish word derived from the German word for "school," since the shul is a place of learning as much as a place of prayer.

Contemporary synagogues vary in many ways: size, organizational structure, the extent to which they conduct nonreligious activities, and the values they reflect. However, because the synagogue remains first and foremost the house of prayer, most synagogues are similar in their physical layout.

The section of the synagogue where prayer services are held is often called the sanctuary. Smaller shuls have no other sections, but many synagogues do have other elements, such as study rooms, banquet halls, or areas for children.

In Orthodox synagogues, the sanctuary is divided, with separate places for men and women. The women may occupy an upper floor, or the side or rear of the first floor, in which case they are separated by a *mechitzah* (wall or curtain).

Since Jews must face in the direction of Jerusalem when praying, synagogues in the United States and Europe are constructed with the front facing east. On the eastern wall is set the *Aron Kodesh* (Holy Ark), in which the Torah scrolls are stored behind an inner curtain called a *parokhet*.

Beyond serving as a house of prayer, a synagogue acts as a *beit midrash* (house of study). In addition to preparation for a bar or bat mitzvah, a synagogue provides opportunities to continue the study of Judaism. A synagogue may also offer social services to the community and sponsor social events.

— 40 —

PRAYER DURING FORMAL WORSHIP

Prayer helps form Judaism's foundation. The origin of the liturgical prayers spoken in synagogues is attributed to the "Men of the Great

Assembly." These are the prophets, sages, scribes, and teachers who, in the centuries after the return from Babylon, continued the work of Ezra and his followers.

Religious observances took place at the Temple in Jerusalem prior to its second destruction two millennia ago. Many of these rituals involved sacrifices. When the First Temple was destroyed and the Babylonian Exile occurred in the sixth century B.C.E., prayer served as a substitute for sacrifice to exiled Jews, though some Jews may have practiced prayer even before that time.

Liturgy is a form of public worship. In Judaism, the liturgy goes back to the days of the Temple. Even after the destruction of the Second Temple, group prayer was considered essential to Judaism, which is why the Jews recite most prayers in the first person plural, "we." If circumstances do not permit otherwise, Judaism encourages a person to pray alone in addition to the customary blessings an individual can make throughout the day. However, in order to conduct a formal public service, a *minyan* is needed.

The prerequisite of a minyan is satisfied with the presence of ten adults, thirteen years of age or older. Orthodox Judaism requires ten men, while Reform and Reconstructionist synagogues allow the number to include women. Conservative congregations vary over gender policies.

Observant Jews pray three times a day in formal worship, and a slew of blessings and prayers can be said individually. The daily prayers follow a basic pattern, with some variation on Shabbat and holidays (and, of course, among the different branches of Judaism).

Shacharit (the morning service) includes morning blessings; *Pesukei D'Zimra* (verses of praise); *Shema* and its blessings; *Shemoneh Esrei*, also known as the *Amidah*; *Musaf* (added on Shabbat and during holidays); *Hallel* (said only on special days); *Ashrei*, *Aleinu*, and other closing prayers, psalms, and hymns (not on Shabbat and holidays).

The *Mincha* is the afternoon service, which consists of the Ashrei, Shemoneh Esrei, and Aleinu. In the evening, the congregation conducts the *Ma'ariv* service. During this time, it recites the Shema, followed by the Shemoneh Esrei and the Aleinu.

Three times each week (Monday, Thursday, and Shabbat) and on holidays, a portion, known as a *parshah,* is read from the Torah. On Shabbat, the *Haftorah* (sometimes *Haftarah*, meaning "concluding portion"), which consists of a passage from the prophets, follows the weekly parshah. There is much ceremony connected with the reading of the Torah as it is removed from the ark, paraded around the sanctuary, and then laid to rest on the *bimah* (pedestal, similar to an altar), where it is read.

Although the Talmud clearly states that one can pray in any language, Hebrew has traditionally been the language for prayer in Judaism. In the past, this tradition was a point of contention, and one of the first changes the Reform movement made was to pray in the vernacular. However, in recent years Hebrew has begun taking a more prominent position in Reform prayer books. As for the Orthodox, Hebrew remains the exclusive language for prayer. Conservative and Reconstructionist liturgies rely on Hebrew to a large extent.

There are several sound reasons as to why Hebrew is the language of choice for prayer, even if people don't understand it. First of all, there is generally an English translation alongside the Hebrew text, so there should be no problem understanding prayers. When people pray in Hebrew, the language strikes a meaningful recognition. It is the language the Jews used thousands of years ago—the same language in which the covenant with God was formed. That is bound to instill strong emotions and raise levels of *kavanah* (spiritual concentration).

But one of the most important justifications for the use of Hebrew in the prayer service is unity. With Jews dispersed to the four corners of the earth, this universal language for prayer has helped preserve Jewish identity. Having the prayers in Hebrew allows any Jew to join any congregation anywhere in the world and be able to pray with fellow Jews.

—— 41 ——

BLESSINGS

According to Jewish tradition, when God chose the Jews to be a holy people, this honor came with the responsibility of making the world a holy place. What better way to demonstrate an appreciation for the world and all therein than to bless each thing and every occasion?

The word *berakhah* (blessing) comes from the Hebrew root *bet-resh-kaf*, from which the word *berech* (knee) is derived. The connection between a blessing and a knee has to do with the practice in prayer services of bending the knee and bowing when reciting a berakhah, a gesture that demonstrates respect.

In addition to the *birkhot* (blessings) that are contained in formal prayer services, there are blessings that are appropriate for almost every daily occurrence, beginning with waking in the morning and ending with going to sleep at night. Birkhot generally fall into one of three categories: those said before enjoying a material pleasure, such as eating or drinking (*birkhot hanehenin*); those recited before performing a mitzvah, such as lighting candles (*birkhot ha-mitzvot*); and those said at special times and events, such as seeing a rainbow or hearing thunder (*birkhot hoda'ah*).

By acquainting yourself with the numerous birkhot and reciting them when appropriate, you can go through each and every day adding a dimension of spirituality to your life and the world in which you live.

All birkhot begin with the phrase, "*barukh atah adonai, elokaynu melekh ha-olam*," which means, "Blessed art Thou Lord, our God, King of the Universe." However, making a blessing does not mean that you are blessing God. In fact, by saying a berakhah, you are acknowledging the wonder of God and the World God created.

— 42 —

IMPORTANT THINGS TO KNOW WHEN
ATTENDING A JEWISH SERVICE

Mavin is the Yiddish word for "expert," or "knowledgeable person." While the material in this section may not make you a mavin at the prayer service, it should help you feel at home—which is exactly how you should feel in a Jewish house of worship.

The word *siddur* means "order" or "arrangement," and the *Siddur* is a prayer book that includes daily prayers, the liturgy of the Shabbat service, and special prayers for various holidays. The Siddur is based on a collection of prayers compiled centuries ago in an academy in Babylon. Naturally, there have been additions and amendments since then, as well as differing styles among various communities and branches of Judaism.

Since this single volume contains the prayers for all the daily services, Shabbat, and some festivals, make sure you know which service you are attending so you can get to the right section. Unfortunately, the sections do not always appear in the exact order in which they are recited, and you may find yourself flipping back and forth between the pages. Normally, the prayer leader will guide the congregants, but this is not always the case, particularly with the Orthodox. If you get lost, don't be afraid to ask somebody to help you find your place.

During prayer service, you will generally be required to make three basic responses. There is the customary "amen" (translated from Hebrew as "so be it"). *Amen* is an affirmation, and it should be said with intensity. When someone says, "*barukh atah adonai*" ("blessed is the Lord"), others rejoin, "*barukh hu u'varukh shemo*" ("blessed is He and blessed is His Name"). Finally, whenever someone recites, "*barukhu et adonai ha-m'vorakh*" ("bless the Lord, the Blessed One"), the congregation responds, "*barukh adonai ha-m'vorakh l'olam va-ed*" ("blessed is the Lord, the Blessed One, forever and ever").

There's a good deal of standing during a Jewish service, so when you see the congregation rising, follow their lead. Generally, people will rise when the ark is open, when the Torah is being carried around the room, during the Shemoneh Esrei, and while the Aleinu is recited. In most congregations the rabbi will tell you when to rise and when to sit. In those very observant congregations where this may not happen, just follow the people on either side of you.

At specific times during a Jewish service, you are expected to bow. To do so properly, you must first bend the knees, then bend forward while straightening the knees, then return to the standing position. It's something like diving into a pool of water, except your arms don't move since you're holding the Siddur.

Whenever there is a Torah reading, the Torah is paraded about, giving the congregants an opportunity to kiss this holy scroll. When the Torah passes, you can touch the cover with your hand, Siddur, or *tallit* (prayer shawl), and then kiss your hand or the object that had just touched the Torah. This action will demonstrate your reverence for the Torah, the holiest object in Judaism.

There are no mitzvot directing synagogue attire. Obviously, you should dress modestly, particularly if you attend an Orthodox synagogue—exercise your common sense and good taste. However, commandments do exist about specific articles of clothing, like the *tefillin* and *kippot* (skullcaps), which should be worn in synagogue during prayer services.

43

ITEMS FOUND IN THE SYNAGOGUE

Idolatry in any form is anathema to Judaism. However, this is not to say that Judaism is without special objects, apparel, and symbols, which you will find in the synagogue as well as in Jewish homes.

The Torah scrolls, which comprise the five books of Moses, are kept in a cabinet known as the Holy Ark. A specially trained scribe known as a *sofer* handwrites the scrolls using a special method of handwriting with *crowns* (stylistic embellishments that look like crows' feet over the upper points of the letters). The text of the Torah includes neither vowels nor musical notes. Those who would like to read the Torah during the services must therefore become skilled in reading the script as well as knowing the appropriate chant melodies.

The scrolls themselves are parchments, prepared from the skin of a kosher animal. You will never have the opportunity to touch this parchment with your hand—if you are reading from the Torah scrolls, you must follow the text with a silver pointer called a *yad* (hand), which makes sense because the yad is in the shape of a hand with a pointing index finger.

Special ornaments adorning the Torah scrolls must be removed before they can be read. This process of "undressing" the Torah involves removing the crowns, the yad, the breastplate, and the mantle. The Torah scrolls are read from a raised platform, known as the *bimah*, located in the center or at the front of the sanctuary. In Sephardic synagogues, the bimah is called the *teyvah* and the Holy Ark is known as the *heichal*. Once the reading is complete and the Torah has been dressed, it is returned to the ark where other sacred objects are stored.

Just above and in front of the ark you will find the *ner tamid* (eternal lamp). In Exodus 27:20–21, God ordained that a burning light be maintained at all times outside the curtain that conceals the Ark of the Covenant.

Because there is no similar mitzvah to keep a menorah, it is not always present in synagogues. The word *menorah* comes from the Hebrew word for "candelabrum." It first appears in Exodus 25 (and later in Exodus 37) in a detailed description of a seven-branched gold candelabrum fashioned by artisan Bezalel for the tabernacle in the wilderness, where the Jews who wandered in the desert prayed to God. Much later, long after the Jews entered the Promised Land, they built the Temple in Jerusalem and priests placed the Temple Menorah there.

Modern menorahs in synagogues symbolize that original menorah in the Temple, but they cannot be exact replicas of the Temple Menorah (for reasons of deference). Consequently, synagogue menorahs frequently have six or eight branches (instead of seven) or, at the very least, a different design than that of the Temple Menorah.

— 44 —

"LAYING" TEFILLIN

Putting on *tefillin* is a mitzvah that appears in four different places in the Written Torah, which commands: "And you shall bind them as a sign on your hand, and they shall be as frontlets between your eyes." Jews fulfill this commandment by "laying" tefillin. Tefillin consist of two cases with small pieces of parchment that contain the four portions in the Torah (Exodus 13:1–10 and 11–16; Deuteronomy 6:4–9 and 11:13–21) in which the Jews receive the commandment to wear tefillin. During prayer, these cases are bound on the arm and head with special leather straps.

The importance of tefillin in prayer services is manifested by the word itself, which is derived from the Hebrew word *tefillah* (prayer). Sometimes tefillin is translated as "phylacteries," a word that derives from the Greek for "protection" or "fortress." However, you should generally refrain from using this term. Many Jews find it offensive because this title assumes that tefillin are nothing more than amulets to ward off evil spirits.

Observant Jews wear tefillin only for morning prayer services that do not fall on the Sabbath and during major holidays like Yom Kippur. Why not lay tefillin on the Sabbath, which is such a holy day? The procedure of laying tefillin is so intricate it requires great concentration. As a Jew places tefillin on his head, arm, and hand, his mundane preoccupations and everyday concerns dissipate, and he begins to pray with a clear head. However, this step is entirely unnecessary on Shabbat, when his head should already be cleared from distractions of everyday life.

The best way to learn about putting on tefillin is to go to a synagogue during a weekday morning service and ask someone to teach you. You will have no problem finding an eager instructor, particularly at Orthodox shuls, where all men know how to do this.

— 45 —

WHY DO JEWS WEAR SKULLCAPS, PRAYER SHAWLS, AND TASSELS?

Many customs and traditions are associated with the way observant Jewish men and women dress. There are some specific items that Jewish people must wear in synagogue.

A *kippah* (Hebrew) or *yarmulke* (Yiddish) is a skullcap worn in the synagogue. The word *yarmulke* comes from the Tartar (via Polish). However, some rabbis believe this word is actually derived from the Aramaic *yerai malkla*, meaning "respect for the Sovereign." The word *kippah* comes from the Hebrew for "head covering."

Wearing a kippah during prayer is an ancient Jewish practice. During the early Middle Ages, rabbis began to instruct Jewish men not to go about bareheaded. The Reform Jews eliminated this custom entirely but later reinstated the practice of wearing kippot in the temple.

There are no mitzvot for wearing a kippah, but it has become a distinctly Jewish tradition. Many Jewish men, particularly the Orthodox, wear a kippah at all times as a reminder that they are always before God and as a sign of respect to Him. Women are not required to wear a kippah, but some congregations require married women to cover their heads. In such instances, a piece of lace is generally provided, or a woman may don a kippah.

Tallit is the Hebrew word for "prayer shawl." The biblical basis for wearing a tallit is found in Numbers 15:37–41, where God instructs Moses to tell the Children of Israel to make *tzitzit* (tassels) on each corner of the tallit and on the corners of their clothing. Tzitzit remind the devout of God's commandments.

The tallit is worn during prayer in the synagogue and at home. Wearing a tallit during prayer is a mitzvah commanded to Jewish men. Women need not wear a tallit, although some congregations permit or even recommend this practice.

The tzitzit are highly symbolic and are made in accordance with very specific configurations. The Kabbalists engaged in all sorts of esoteric practices with the number of knots, double knots, and windings of the tzitzit. They counted thirty-nine windings in each fringe and derived an identical numerical value with the phrase *adonai echad* ("the Lord is one," the end of the Shema prayer).

46

JUDAIC DECORATIONS: THE STAR OF DAVID, THE CHAI, AND THE HAMESH

Although Jews are not commanded to "advertise" their Jewishness (except, perhaps, by wearing a kippah or tzitzit—see number 45), some Jews like to demonstrate their beliefs or heritage by adorning themselves with certain symbolic objects.

The most popular symbol of Judaism is the *magen david* (the six-pointed Star of David), though there exists no proof whatsoever to substantiate the fact that the magen david has anything to do with King David. Indeed, it is very unlikely that the magen david dates back all the way to biblical times.

No one can say with any certainty just when the magen david first appeared. By the seventeenth century, it had become a popular symbol for adorning synagogues. When the Zionist movement adopted the magen david as its emblem at the end of the nineteenth century, it became the universal symbol to represent Judaism and the Jewish people. Today, it is part of the flag of the modern state of Israel.

Another symbol that appears on necklaces and other jewelry is the *chai*. The chai consists of the two Hebrew letters, *chet* and *yud,* which make up the word for "life" or "living." The chai's significance has to do with the value Judaism places upon life.

A less likely choice in terms of jewelry that represents Judaism, but one that is usually found in Jewish gift shops, is the *hamesh* (or *hamsa*), an inverted hand with the thumb and pinkie pointed outward. The hamesh hand is also found in Arab cultures and may originally have become popular as an amulet.

— 47 —

THE MEZUZAH AND OTHER RELIGIOUS ITEMS FOUND IN JEWISH HOMES

What you find in a Jewish home depends, of course, upon how observant the family is as well as on what branch of Judaism they follow.

The *mezuzah* is something commonly found in many Jewish homes. Affixing a mezuzah on the doorpost is more than a Jewish tradition. This practice is mandated by the commandment found in Deuteronomy 6:4–9 (the Shema): "And thou shalt write them upon the doorposts of thy house and upon thy gates." This passage, along with a portion from Deuteronomy 11:13–21, is inscribed on a tiny scroll (the *klaf*), as part of the mezuzah, and housed in a small case. The container is usually wooden, ceramic, or metal, and contains the letter *shin* (the first letter of *El Shaddai*, "God Almighty").

Implicit in the act of affixing a mezuzah to the doorpost is the sentiment that the spirit of Godliness will permeate the home and all who reside therein. Furthermore, the words in the mezuzah resonate with the central precepts of Judaism—the unity of God, the love of God, the importance of tradition, and the transmittal of these values to one's children. Following precepts in the Talmud, some Jewish families affix a mezuzah to the doorpost of each room (except the bathroom and kitchen). When leaving or entering the house, many Jews will touch the mezuzah and then kiss the fingers that touched it.

Since a mezuzah must be treated with reverence, you should take it with you when you move. However, if you know that a Jewish family is moving in and that it will be treated with respect, you should leave it attached.

Beyond the mezuzah, the following list includes some common religious objects you might encounter:

- **Hanukkah menorah:** These menorahs have nine branches and are used in celebrations of Hanukkah (see number 64).
- **Shabbat candles:** Families who observe the Shabbat light candles just before Shabbat commences (see number 51).
- **Kiddush cup:** A wine glass or chalice used for reciting the *Kiddush* (a prayer that sanctifies the Shabbat or a particular holiday—see number 51).
- **Spice box.** This object is used in the ceremony of the *Havdalah*, which marks the end of Shabbat (see number 51).
- **Challah cover:** A cloth used to cover *challah* (special Shabbat bread) and other types of food, especially during holiday dinners.

Many Ashkenazic Jewish homes also have a *pushke*, a container used for collecting money in observance of the mitzvah of giving to charities and helping the less fortunate. Members of the family put their spare change, or whatever money they can afford, into the pushke.

Naturally, there are many other articles that can contribute to a Jewish environment in the home, including a Bible and a *Siddur* (prayer book); books about Judaism and Jewish history, philosophy, and culture; and even Jewish art and music.

Part 4
Holy Days
and Festivals

JUDAISM IS UNIQUE IN THAT ITS HOLIEST DAY, *SHABBAT* (THE day of rest), also occurs the most frequently, once every seven days. But there are many other Jewish holy days and festivals. The Days of Awe, which include Rosh Hashanah and Yom Kippur, are the only other occasions considered nearly as consecrated as Shabbat. Unlike most of the other holidays and festivals, Rosh Hashanah and Yom Kippur are primarily observed in the synagogue rather than the home.

The seven-day festival of Sukkot occurs just five days after Yom Kippur, followed by Shemini Atzeret and Simchat Torah. Even though these are holidays laden with history and meaning, they are joyous times of celebration that include jubilant activities and observances.

The festival of Purim is yet another happy occasion, and it is perhaps celebrated with more fun and frolic any other Jewish holiday. And why not, considering that Purim commemorates a historical episode packed with court intrigue, convoluted plots, revelry, and a fascinating cast of characters? Throw in the near annihilation of the Jewish population, and, finally, its deliverance at the hands of a beautiful damsel, and the makings of a triumphant celebration are in order.

The last three holidays in the Jewish calendar's annual cycle are Shavuot (the Festival of Weeks), Tisha B'Av (a day that commemorates the destruction of the Temple), and Tu B'Shevat (a New Year's day for trees). All of these holidays, each in its own way, commemorate Jewish history and culture.

--- 48 ---

OBSERVING SHABBAT

In Judaism, Shabbat is the most important day of the week. In fact, the Jewish tradition considers Shabbat more sacred than Yom Kippur (the Day of Atonement). The Jews received the commandment to observe Shabbat in the Ten Statements, which instructs: "Remember the Sabbath day and keep it holy." This charge, a sign of the covenant between God and the Jewish people, carries a blessing and a responsibility.

God commanded the Jews to "remember" and "to observe" Shabbat (Exodus 20:8 and Deuteronomy 5:12), a two-fold injunction. Halakah and mitzvot having to do with Shabbat serve this purpose.

The word *Shabbat* comes from the Hebrew root *shin-bet-tav*, which carries the meaning of "to rest" or "cessation of labor." Shabbat is also sometimes referred to as "the Queen of the week" or "the Bride," in part because mystics believed the *Shechinah* ("God's Presence," a feminine word) descends each Friday night as the sun sets.

On the seventh day of the week, Jews rest and turn their minds toward prayer and the home. Observant Jewish families gather to welcome the Shabbat and to end it the following evening. This day is central to both Judaism and the Jewish people. According to Achad Ha-Am, a Jewish writer, "More than Israel has kept the Sabbath, the Sabbath has kept Israel."

Naturally, the Orthodox assiduously follow Halakah concerning Shabbat. To a large extent, much of what follows in this section will reflect the Orthodox tradition. However, the different branches of Judaism, all of which observe the Sabbath and encourage their members to do likewise, do not abide by all the interdictions. Some have even added their own unique customs.

In anticipation of Shabbat, the most important step is preparing to receive the Divine Presence and welcome the Sabbath Queen. In other words, Jews are supposed to put themselves in a "Shabbat state of mind." They remove all thoughts of work and everyday concerns; gear up for a time of rest, study, and worship; and look ahead toward a time for togetherness with family, friends, and community.

Other more practical steps include cleaning the house, setting the Shabbat dinner table and preparing the Shabbat meal, bathing, and dressing up for the occasion. These practical and spiritual preparations begin on Friday afternoon, before the holiday commences.

In Judaism, the day does not begin in the middle of the night or with the sunrise, but in the evening, at sunset. Hence, Shabbat begins exactly eighteen minutes before sunset and ends on Saturday night, after three stars appear in the night sky (approximately forty minutes after sunset).

— 49 —

WHY ARE CERTAIN ACTIVITIES PROHIBITED DURING SHABBAT?

As with all Jewish law, there are both prohibitions and affirmative obligations associated with Shabbat, the day of rest. The prohibitions are called the *melachah*, loosely translated to mean "work." A more precise definition would be work that is creative or that exercises dominion over the environment.

Energy expenditure or physical labor is not necessarily the only criteria for melachah. For example, flipping a light switch does not require much energy or effort, but because it is a creative act it is prohibited during Shabbat. There are two underlying explanations regarding the prohibition of turning on a light. The first reason has to do with the interdiction against cooking, which involves heating metal. Second, people are forbidden to build on Shabbat and turning on a light switch completes (or builds) a circuit.

On the other hand, walking up a flight of stairs is permitted. Although it does require an expenditure of energy, it is not a creative act and does not exercise control over the environment.

The rabbis established thirty-nine categories of forbidden acts, which they set forth in the *Mishnah* (the code of Jewish law). Some of these categories include:

- Plowing
- Weaving
- Baking
- Tying
- Slaughtering
- Taking an object from the private domain into the public
- Writing ("creating" words)
- Building
- Kindling a fire
- Hitting with a hammer

In addition to these enjoined activities, Jews observing Shabbat cannot come into contact with any instrument that could be employed for a prohibited purpose, so, for instance, holding an unlit match that could be used to kindle a fire or picking up a pen that could be used to write would be prohibited.

On Shabbat, observant Jews can't turn on a television set (although turning it on before Shabbat and leaving it on would be fine). There's also no hopping into the car to go out for dinner or to see a movie. Since the automobile operates by means of an internal-combustion engine necessitating the burning of gasoline, driving would violate the interdiction against kindling a fire. Also, given the distances normally traveled by car, the prohibition of transporting an object in the public domain would likely be violated as well.

Sabbath restrictions are not meant to punish. Rather, they are intended to remove human beings from the mundane activity of daily life, so they can instead engage in activities that will fill the time in an exceptional way.

— 50 —

SHABBAT SERVICES

While individual prayers and family ceremonies are important in Judaism, community prayer is indispensable. Although much of the Sabbath is celebrated among family and friends, the opportunity to do so with the congregation—"extended family," so to speak—should not be missed. The synagogue affords an excellent setting for the Jewish community to gather together to welcome Shabbat and to reaffirm the covenant with God and with one another.

On the eve of Shabbat, the *kabbalat shabbat* service welcomes the Sabbath. It is followed by the Sabbath evening, or *Ma'ariv* service, with additional prayers. In some synagogues, particularly those that practice Reform Judaism, the main Sabbath service may be held on Friday night. Following services, most Reform and Conservative congregations have an *oneg shabbat* (joy of the Sabbath), where refreshments are available and the congregation has the opportunity to socialize.

On Saturday, Sabbath observances continue with the morning service, which has three parts: *Shacharit* (morning service), the Torah reading, and *Musaf* (additional Shabbat prayer service). Again, following this service there is a *Kiddush* (a blessing) where wine and perhaps cakes and cookies are served. At this time, families can return home to enjoy the rest of Shabbat.

It wouldn't be a surprise to see a Jewish family that drives to a Friday night Shabbat service at their Reform Temple and then goes about their business on Saturday morning. Nor is it odd for families who leave a Conservative synagogue following Saturday morning services to go out to a restaurant for lunch. Families might even go hiking in the woods to take in the beauty of nature or talk in a relaxed atmosphere among themselves on an early Saturday afternoon. No matter the differences among Jews and how they choose to observe Shabbat, all branches hold the Shabbat in high esteem.

51

WHAT DO JEWISH FAMILIES DO DURING SHABBAT?

As the Shabbat begins, the mother of a family will traditionally light two candles, which represent the mitzvot to "remember" and "observe." (Some families follow a slightly different tradition and light a candle for every family member present.) The candles may be any color, but they are usually white. Before lighting the Sabbath candles and welcoming Shabbat, it is also common for families to set aside a sum of money for charity.

Unlike other blessings that take place before the act, the woman of the house first lights the candles (at least eighteen minutes before sunset) and then makes the blessing—to do otherwise would require striking a match on the Sabbath. Then, the man of the house recites the *Kiddush* (blessing) over the wine.

If there is no woman of the house, it is perfectly acceptable for the man of the house to light the candles. Similarly, if there is no man to say the Kiddush, a woman may do this.

The family may then greet each other with the words *shabbat shalom!* (in Hebrew) or *gut shabbes!* (in Yiddish) as the Sabbath has now begun. At this time, some families attend a brief Shabbat service (*kabbalat shabbat*) and then return home for dinner.

The Shabbat dinner is important, and the ambiance should befit the special occasion. It is customary to invite a stranger, traveler, or poor person to be a guest at a Shabbat dinner. On this day, Jewish families use their best china and silverware; people often add a vase filled with fresh flowers and a white tablecloth. The Shabbat dinner table also requires a Kiddush cup, wine or grape juice, two *challahs* (special Shabbat bread loaves) covered with white material, and candles.

Just before dinner, people wash their hands and make a blessing over the challah (this blessing is known as the *motzi*). Another beautiful custom that may take place at the Shabbat dinner table is parents blessing their children.

It is also customary to sprinkle salt over the challah or to dip the challah in salt. One explanation for this custom is that salt was a valuable commodity in Roman times and available only to a free people. Another reason has to do with the fact that ever since the destruction of the Temple, the home has become a small sanctuary with a table and altar. Given that sacrifices were offered with salt, sprinkling salt on the challah is a link to the times of Temple Judaism.

The only requirements for the Sabbath meal are bread and wine. Of course, the food is subject to the laws of kashrut and may not be cooked once the Shabbat begins. Traditional foods found at the Ashkenazic Shabbat table include gefilte fish, chopped liver, chicken soup with matzah balls or noodles, roast chicken or brisket of beef, and noodle or potato kugel. Among Sephardic Jews, customary meals may consist of fish, eggplant salad, lamb roast, stuffed grape leaves, and white rice.

Shabbat dinner is the time for a family to have deeper conversations. During or after the meal, some families will sing Sabbath songs. At the meal's conclusion, the *birkat ha-mazon* (the grace after meals) is recited.

It's customary to eat three meals during the Sabbath. *Sholosh seudot*, or *seudah shelishit* (the third meal), generally takes place in the late afternoon. While there is no Kiddush, hands must be washed and the motzi blessing recited over two loaves of challah. Since it is understandable that the family may not be terribly hungry at this time, a light meal is typically served.

In addition to attending synagogue services on Shabbat, people get involved in other activities to bring a special dimension to this festive day. Most activities revolve around praying, reading, and studying. Naturally, the congregation performs a public reading of the Torah during the

Saturday morning services, but readings from the Talmud and religious discussions may follow later on that day, whether at the synagogue or at home.

But things need not always be so serious. Some people play games, take family walks, or engage in other leisure activities. The point is for people to remove themselves from the ordinary and enter the holiness of Shabbat.

Shabbat ends at nightfall when three stars appear in the night sky, usually about forty minutes after sunset. At this time, the family performs the *Havdalah* (separation) ceremony. During Havdalah, blessings are made over the wine, a specially woven or braided multiwick havdalah candle, and a box called a *bsamim*, which contains sweet-smelling spices. Each object represents something:

- The wine cup is filled to the brim, expressing hope that the upcoming week will be filled with divine blessings.
- Blazing like a torch, the havdalah candle's flame signifies light and guidance through life.
- The spices remind the devout to make an effort to bring some of the sweetness of Shabbat into the coming week.

This is a great opportunity to include children in ceremony activity, by having them hold the candle and the spice box. At this time, the family recites the final blessing regarding the division between the consecrated and the worldly, which reflects how the Sabbath is distinct from the other days of the week.

52

SEEKING FORGIVENESS AND RECONCILIATION DURING THE DAYS OF AWE

The annual cycle of Jewish holidays begins with the Days of Awe, a ten-day period that generally falls sometime in September or October. The Days of Awe begin with *Rosh Hashanah* (the Jewish New Year—see numbers 53 and 54) and end with *Yom Kippur* (the Day of Atonement—see numbers 55, 56, and 57), the most solemn and introspective day of the year.

The Days of Awe are the time of the year when people make a concerted effort to engage in *teshuva*. The Hebrew word for "turning" or "returning," teshuva refers to the act of repentance. In fact, this ten-day period is known as *Yamim Noraim* (Days of Repentence).

According to Jewish tradition, all people have the capacity to do good and evil. Every day, each person faces choices between right and wrong. Judaism recognizes that people are not perfect and they make mistakes. These mistakes may be corrected through teshuvah, which implies turning or returning to God. Teshuvah begins with an intense examination of one's actions and the desire and intent to strive toward being a better person.

During the Days of Awe, Jews seek forgiveness for their sins, but individually they also make an effort to become better people. They are expected to seek reconciliation with others and request forgiveness for any sins committed against them. Judaism teaches that, although God will forgive sins committed against Him, if you act unjustly toward another person, you must seek that person's forgiveness.

According to tradition, God has a heavenly ledger known as *Sefer Ha-Chayyim* (The Book of Life). During the Days of Repentance, He writes down the names of those who will have a good life and those who will not, as well as those who will live and those who will die in the ensuing year. He opens the Book of Life on Rosh Hashanah and closes it at the conclusion of Yom Kippur. It is believed that people's actions during this period can alter the initial determination. Hence, in addition to *tefillah* (prayer) and performing acts of *tzedakah* (good deeds and charity), teshuvah is important in trying to affect an individual's life over the course of the next year.

In addition to Rosh Hashanah and Yom Kippur, other special days take place during the Days of Awe. On the third day, observant Jews participate in a minor fast known as *Tzom Gedaliah*. This fast marks the assassination of the last governor of Judea after the destruction of the First Temple. The Sabbath that occurs during the Ten Days of Repentance is known as *Shabbat Shuvah*, the Sabbath of Return. A special Haftorah is read, and a rather lengthy sermon about repentance is often given from the books of the Prophets, Hosea, Micah, and Joel.

— 53 —

ROSH HASHANAH: THE JEWISH NEW YEAR

Rosh Hashanah (head of the year) is commonly known as the Jewish New Year. This Jewish holiday, which commences the Days of Awe, commemorates the creation of the world. Most Reform Jews and Jews living in Israel celebrate Rosh Hashanah for one day, but the other branches of Judaism observe Rosh Hashanah for two days.

In Leviticus 23:24–25, it is written that on the first day of the seventh month, there "shall be a solemn rest unto you, a memorial proclaimed with the blast of horns, a holy convocation. . . ."

Later, in Numbers 29:1, it is proclaimed that this day shall be a "holy day," a day when Jews should not work, and a day when "the shofar is trumpeted." (The *shofar* is a ram's horn, blown particularly at synagogue services during the High Holidays.) The Torah only refers to Rosh Hashanah as *Yom Teruah* (the day of the sounding of the shofar) or *Yom Ha-Zikaron* (the day of remembrance). Yom Ha-Zikaron is a reference to Abraham's willingness to sacrifice his only son, Isaac, in demonstration of his unswerving obedience to God.

The phrase "Rosh Hashanah" emerged during the Talmudic times (the first five centuries C.E.). However, the holiday itself was well established by the fourth century B.C.E., after the Babylonian exile when some Jews had returned to Jerusalem to construct the Second Temple.

Given the importance of this period, preparations for the Days of

Awe begin in the preceding month of Elul, when it is customary to blow the shofar during weekly synagogue services. It is considered a great honor to blow the shofar, which is no ordinary ram's horn.

As the month of Elul draws to an end, there is a special *Selichot* (forgiveness) service on the Saturday night before Rosh Hashanah, when the congregation recites a series of important prayers. Around midnight, the congregation reviews the thirteen attributes of God (see number 24), a ceremony that helps to prepare everyone for the approaching holy days.

During this season of the New Year, it is customary to send *Shanah Tovah* (good year) cards to friends and family. It's also important to have certain items and food necessary for Rosh Hashanah, including holiday candlesticks and candles; wine, a decanter, and wine cups; two round *challahs* (special bread); challah cover; a holiday bread knife; cut or sliced apples; honey; and flowers.

Rosh Hashanah begins a new calendar year, but there are three other "new year" celebrations in the Jewish tradition: Nisan, the month in which Passover occurs, begins the counting of the calendar months and counting the reign of kings; Elul, the month preceding Rosh Hashanah, is the symbolic new year for tithing animals, a form of charity; and Tu B'Shevat, the fifteenth day of Shevat, is the new year for trees.

54

Rosh Hashanah ceremonies, customs, and services

Since Rosh Hashanah is an important holiday, it is customary to follow the Torah principle of *Hiddur Mitzvah*, which requires taking additional time and effort to make the ritual more beautiful and exceptional. Hence, the list of necessary things is similar to what you would use for the Shabbat dinner—including your best dishes, glassware, fine linen, and fresh flowers.

Just as on Shabbat and other holidays, two candles are lit to welcome Rosh Hashanah, and the mother of the household recites two special blessings. Then, the father says the Kiddush prayer and a special blessing over the wine or grape juice. The motzi is made over two loaves of challah bread, which are made round especially for Rosh Hashanah. Incidentally, challah is round on Rosh Hashanah, to symbolize a crown and remind the Jewish people of God's sovereignty. The round challah also represents the circle of life that will continue for eternity.

Although there are no special menus designated for the Rosh Hashanah dinner, traditional meals are similar to Shabbat dinners and include apples and honey. Dipping apples in honey is symbolic of having a sweet new year. Honey is also spread over bread or included in recipes such as honey cakes, or *tzimmes*, a sweet stew of carrots, cinnamon, yams, and prunes. There is also a custom of making a brief prayer and eating a number of symbolic foods such as carrots, leeks or cabbage, beets, dates, gourds, pomegranates, and fish.

Rosh Hashanah is a day of rest, and much of the time is spent in a synagogue. Three central prayers dominate the Rosh Hashanah services: *Avinu Malkeinu, Unetaneh Tokef,* and the *Musaf Amidah.* It is during the Musaf Amidah that the *shofar* (ram's horn) is sounded. These prayers begin somewhat earlier in the morning and last into the early afternoon. In addition to these prayers, the congregation reads a portion of the Torah. On the first day, one of the readings has to do with the birth of Isaac (Abraham and Sarah's son). On the second day, the Torah portion recounts Isaac's halted sacrifice.

Tashlikh (casting off) is a popular activity during the afternoon of the first day of Rosh Hashanah. The ritual involves walking to a body of water, reciting designated prayers, and then emptying one's pockets or tossing breadcrumbs into the water. This ceremony symbolizes casting-off sins. Should the first day of Rosh Hashanah occur on Shabbat, Tashlikh is postponed until the next day. (As always, Shabbat takes precedence over any other day.)

Many people visit the graves of their loved ones during this season. While people probably have other reasons for carrying on this custom today, it likely originated with the belief that the thoughts or prayers of the deceased can intercede in heaven on behalf of the living. Obviously, such assistance would be particularly welcome during the Days of Awe, when repentance is foremost in people's mind.

55

YOM KIPPUR: THE DAY OF ATONEMENT

Yom Kippur is the "Day of Atonement," a day when Jews atone for their sins of the prior year. Sometimes referred to as the "Sabbath of Sabbaths," Yom Kippur has been an integral part of Judaism for thousands of years.

The last of the Days of Awe, Yom Kippur is observed on the tenth of *Tishri*, the seventh month of the Jewish calendar. While Shabbat is the holiest of days, it's human nature to regard Yom Kippur, which occurs only once a year as opposed to once a week, as something very special. That's why even those Jews who never attend a Shabbat service during the rest of the year often go to synagogue on Yom Kippur.

The first Yom Kippur occurred at the time Moses received the Ten Statements at Mount Sinai (see number 21). Returning to the base of the mountain, and upon seeing the Hebrews worshipping a golden calf, Moses destroyed the original Ten Statements. Later, when Moses ascended Mount Sinai for the second time, the Hebrews fasted from sunrise to sunset, praying for forgiveness. On the tenth day of Tishri, Moses returned with the second set of the Ten Statements. Having found that the Hebrews were truly repentant, Moses announced that God had forgiven them.

Thus, in Leviticus 16:29–31, it is written that every year on the tenth day of Tishri "you must fast and do no work. . . . This is because on this day you shall have all your sins atoned. . . . It is a Sabbath of Sabbaths to you. . . . This is a law for all time."

It doesn't get any clearer than this. For thousands of years, Jews have refrained from work, instead fasting, praying, and doing everything in their power to fulfill the obligation to honor this "Sabbath of Sabbaths."

Over the centuries, Jews have observed Yom Kippur in different ways. For example, in biblical times, the high priest sacrificed animals as an offering to seek forgiveness for sins. Later, the high priest of the Temple atoned ritually for the sins of the Hebrews by symbolically placing them on two goats—one to be sacrificed and the other sent to its death in the wilderness. (It is said that this is the origin for the word "scapegoat.")

Another ancient practice involved the custom of *kapparot* (atonements), which occurred on the afternoon before Yom Kippur. A live chicken was swung around a person's head while a special prayer was recited. The chicken was then slaughtered and given to the poor, or else a donation was made to a charity. Though not common, very observant Jews and many Sephardim (both religious and secular) living in Israel still follow this practice.

Today, God's forgiveness is sought through prayers of penitence and fasting. People also pursue other introspective activities, to help them accomplish teshuvah and lead a better life.

56

WHICH ACTIVITIES ARE PROHIBITED ON YOM KIPPUR?

Most people, even non-Jews, know that eating and drinking is forbidden on Yom Kippur. The fast commences before sunset on the evening of Yom Kippur and ends after nightfall the next day.

Jews should only observe the mitzvah to fast as long as it does not pose a physical threat. Children under the age of nine and women in childbirth (that is, from the time the labor commences to three days following the birth) are absolutely not permitted to fast. Older children and women from the third to the seventh day after childbirth are permitted to fast, but should resume eating or drinking if they feel the need.

There is no need to have a reason to fast. It is a mitzvah from God that appears in the Torah. However, many rationales have been offered in this regard. For one, refraining from consuming food or liquid is a concrete expression of the gravity of the day. It helps each person attain the state of mind required to focus on the spiritual. Furthermore, fasting manifests a form of self-mastery over bodily needs. Another more socially conscious justification states that by fasting, people can identify more readily with the poor and the hungry. Any of these reasons, or any one that is personally meaningful to an individual, will do. Whatever the reasons, fasting is fundamental to the observance of Yom Kippur.

But fasting is only one of five prohibitions that must be obeyed during Yom Kippur.

The other prohibitions are:

- No washing or bathing
- No using creams and oils (a prohibition that extends to deodorants and cosmetics)
- No having sexual relations
- No wearing leather shoes

One reason for not wearing leather shoes is the incongruity of deriving a benefit from the slaying of one of God's creatures while praying and beseeching God for a long life. This proscription might explain why it's not uncommon to see men wearing formal suits and canvas sneakers on Yom Kippur.

--- *57* ---

YOM KIPPUR PREPARATIONS AND SERVICES

Many activities are involved in preparing for Yom Kippur. On the day before this holiday, Jews recite the *viddui* (confessional) during afternoon prayers. It is customary for men to wear white during all Yom Kippur services, because it is believed it enhances the mood. More observant men often wear a *kittel*, a white ankle-length robe, over their clothes. The rabbi and cantor also wear white robes. The Torah scrolls are dressed in white, and the table on which the Torah is read is covered in white. Even the *parokhet curtains* (the curtains inside the Holy Ark, where the Torah scrolls are stored) are white.

In anticipation of Yom Kippur, preparations are also made for the final meal before the twenty-five-hour fast, the *Seudah Ha-Mafseket*. While there are no absolute requirements concerning what you should eat or drink at this time, the meal is traditionally similar to what is served on Shabbat, although the Kiddush is not recited (see number 51).

The liturgy for Yom Kippur (and Rosh Hashanah) is so extensive that a special prayer book, known as the *machzor*, exists specifically for these services. The Yom Kippur services begin in the evening, with a special service before the main service called the *Kol Nidre* (all vows), named for the prayer with which it begins. The Kol Nidre prayer is chanted with a haunting melody. The prayer itself, a legal formula, was written in Aramaic and renders null and void all promises that are made to God but will not be kept in the ensuing year. (However, the Kol Nidre does not apply to promises made to other persons.) Kol Nidre is also considered to be a declaration by worshippers that they should not be held liable for oaths made either in anger or under duress.

Following the Kol Nidre service is the customary *Ma'ariv* evening service including a special confessional prayer called *Amidah*. The Ma'ariv is chanted in a melody reserved for Yom Kippur. After Ma'ariv, it is time to go home to prepare for the full day of prayers (without nourishment) that lies ahead.

The *Shacharit* (morning service) is similar to most morning services held on festivals, except that extra poems are recited and the *Shacharit Amidah* includes a confessional. The congregation reads a portion of the Torah and then a Haftorah from Isaiah (57:14–58:14), a passage critical of those who fast without having a true understanding of the day. A special memorial prayer, called *Yizkor*, is recited for those who have lost their relatives, particularly their parents.

Then the congregation goes on to the lengthy additional *Musaf* service. The two high points of the Musaf are the *Avodah* and the *Eleh Ezkerah* portions of the service. In contrast to the length of the Musaf, the traditional afternoon service, the *Mincha*, is the shortest on this holy day. As you can see, Jews can easily spend the entire day in synagogue, although most congregations take a break after the Musaf to allow families to go home for a rest.

Neilah concludes the Yom Kippur service. During the entire service, which lasts about an hour, the ark is kept open and the congregation must remain standing. The Hebrew word *neilah* means "locked," and symbolizes the closing of the gates of heaven. Neilah ends with a very long blast from the *shofar* (ram's horn). Once Yom Kippur has concluded, families hasten home for the break-the-fast meal.

Throughout the Yom Kippur liturgy, all sins are confessed in the plural, using "we" and "us." This is because Judaism sees the individual in terms of a greater group and holds the belief that each person should assume responsibility for the entire community.

58

THE SIGNIFICANCE OF SUKKOT

The word *sukkot* is Hebrew for "booths," and Sukkot is known as the Festival of Booths or the Feast of Tabernacles. In biblical times, Sukkot was considered the most important festival and was simply referred to as *ha-chag* (the festival). Sukkot, along with Passover and Shavu'ot, are the three pilgrimage festivals, known as *shalosh regalim*, commanded in the Bible. During these festivals, the Hebrews made pilgrimages to the Temple in Jerusalem. But this holiday has deeper origins, reaching back beyond the days of the Temple.

Sukkot has its historical roots in the time the Hebrews wandered in the wilderness for forty years as punishment for refusing to enter the Promised Land after spies delivered a deceitful report claiming the inhabitants were too fierce to be overcome. (Appropriately enough, the forty years in the desert correspond to the forty days the spies spent in Canaan.)

To help ensure that the Hebrews could survive in the desert, God created "clouds of glory" around the Hebrews to protect them from the harsh elements. The Hebrews lived in temporary dwellings, or booths, represented today by the *sukkah* (singular of *sukkot*, which means a "booth" or a "tent"). To ensure that the Jews would never forget this part of their history, God commanded in Leviticus 23:42–43: "You shall live in booths seven days in order that future generations may know that I made the Israelite people live in booths when I brought them out of the land of Egypt."

Historically, Sukkot is also a harvest festival, sometimes referred to as *Chag Ha-Asif* (the Festival of the Ingathering). This holiday marked the end of the harvest, when farmers completed their work and traveled to the Temple in Jerusalem with their families to celebrate and offer their gratitude for a good harvest. During this time, they resided in booths.

In Exodus 23:16, Torah teaches the Hebrews to celebrate the festival of ingathering when they "gather in" the results of their labors. In Deuteronomy 16:13, God instructs the Hebrews to celebrate the Feast of Booths for seven days after the harvest.

Furthermore, this holiday reminds the Jews of those days of wandering in the desert and how God protected them with the clouds of glory that enveloped the Hebrews from above, below, and all around—just as the sukkah surrounds people when they enter it. Spending time in a *sukkah* can serve as a reminder to all Jews that everything they have, including the shelter they live in, ultimately comes from God.

Keep in mind that, unlike more somber Jewish holidays, Sukkot is a holiday meant for having a good time. In fact, this festival is sometimes referred to as *Zeman Simkhateinu*, or the "Season of Our Rejoicing."

— 59 —

Building and using a sukkah

As explained in number 58, the central custom and mitzvah of Sukkot is to dwell in a *sukkah*, a booth or temporary structure. In constructing a sukkah, Jews must follow specific requirements.

The sukkah structure must be at least three feet high and at least twenty-six inches in length and width. The walls cannot exceed thirty feet in height (although some sources specify that they may be as tall as forty feet). The sukkah may be constructed from cinder blocks, lumber, canvas or nylon sheeting attached to a frame of wood, metal piping, or any other suitable material.

The rules governing the *sekhakh* (covering) are very explicit; following these rules will ensure that the sukkah is kosher. Because the sukkah is meant to be a booth, the sekhakh must be temporary, and the material allowed for its construction is limited. Only organic material grown from the ground that is no longer attached to the ground can be used. Hence, wood of all kinds, such as leafy branches and evergreens, are usually acceptable, while metal, plastic, and glass may not be used.

The sekhakh must be spaced evenly, with gaps no wider than eleven and a half inches, so that the covering is ample enough to provide shade. Furthermore, the boards or beams used should be no wider than sixteen inches, so that people inside can still see the stars at night.

However, there are exemptions to sukkah duty. For example, if sitting inside the sukkah causes physical discomfort—for instance, if it's raining heavily or you're under attack by killer bees—you don't have to remain in the sukkah. However, in the event of inclement weather that's not severe, the obligation to spend time in the sukkah remains. If it does rain, more material should not be added to fill in the gaps on the sekhakh, because then the sukkah will no longer be kosher.

The Talmud includes a number of suggestions for decorating a sukkah: hanging carpets and tapestries, nuts and almonds, peaches and grape branches, and wreaths made from ears of corn. More contemporary decorations include fruits, Indian corn, pictures of Jerusalem and other Jewish symbols or works of art (especially those made by your own family), and New Year's greeting cards.

Many Jews invite guests to their sukkah, to fulfill the mitzvah of hospitality (*hachnasat orechim*). In accordance with another custom, called *Ushpizin*, seven symbolic biblical guests are invited to the sukkah each day. These guests are Abraham, Isaac, Jacob, Joseph, Moses, Aaron, and David. Recently, some Jews have begun extending this invitation to female biblical figures, such as Sarah, Rachel, Rebecca, Leah, Miriam, Abigail, and Esther.

The mitzvot of Sukkot also require that meals be eaten inside the sukkah. In fact, today, this is the sukkah's primary function. There is a special obligation to eat in the sukkah on the first night of the holiday, even if it is raining. However, the elderly and sick, as well as mothers with small children, are not required to eat meals in the sukkah.

There are a few other exceptions. For one, a bride and groom are exempt from dwelling in a sukkah. And when people are traveling they are not required to locate a sukkah in which to have their meals.

Before eating any food in the sukkah, a holiday blessing must be made. It is customary to visit friends, travel from sukkah to sukkah and make Kiddush if partaking of a festival meal. A blessing must also be made before sitting in the sukkah. And like Shabbat, each time people eat a meal they must say a blessing for washing the hands, and the motzi over the bread. There is another special blessing when eating food made from the five grains or when drinking wine. As with all holidays, Sukkot is welcomed with the lighting of candles on the night it begins.

At times when it's difficult for Jews to construct a traditional sukkah (for instance, when living in an apartment where there is no backyard) people can do other things, such as designating an area inside the home as a symbolic sukkah and spending time decorating and then dwelling in that space. Or some people establish a holiday table where they place a miniature sukkah as a centerpiece and add other adornments. At any rate, most Jews have access to a communal sukkah that they can use to fulfill this special mitzvah.

— 60 —

SUKKOT SERVICES AND LITURGY

While Sukkot is best known for what occurs outside the synagogue, in the sukkah (booth), the services and liturgy are significant and distinctive. During Sukkot, readings are taken from the biblical book of Ecclesiastes (Kohelet).

The congregation follows each morning's *Amidah* with *Hallel* (psalms of praise). Hymns asking God for forgiveness are also recited during morning services. These hymns are known as *Hoshanot* because they all begin with the Hebrew word *hoshanu* (save us).

Hoshanot are chanted while parading in a procession (except on Shabbat, when the congregants recite the hoshanot while standing beside their seats) and serve as a reminder of similar processions during the time of the Temple. All Hoshanot but one were composed by Rabbi Elazar Hakallir during the Middle Ages.

Then there is the Four Species (*arba minim*), which has to do with one of the mitzvot associated with Sukkot. In Leviticus 23:40, it is written God commanded that on the first day of the festival, "You shall take the product of goodly trees, branches of palm trees, boughs of leafy trees, and willows of the brook, and you will rejoice before the Lord your God seven days."

The Four Species include an *etrog* (a member of the citrus family native to Israel that resembles a lemon), a *lulav* (a dried palm branch), *aravot* (two willow branches), and *hadasim* (three myrtle branches). The lulav, aravot, and hadasim are bound together in a specific manner and referred to collectively as the lulav.

The lulav and etrog come into use twice during the service. During the Hallel prayer, members of the congregation shake and wave the Four Species. During the Hoshanot processions, conducted every day of Sukkot (except Shabbat), people hold the lulav and etrog in hand, shaking and waving them in all directions, actions that symbolize God's omnipresence.

On the seventh day of Sukkot, the procession makes seven circuits around the *bimah* (the pedestal where the Torah scroll is placed during Torah readings). Therefore, this last day of Sukkot is known as *Hoshanah Rabbah* (the Great Hoshanah).

According to the Jewish tradition, the Four Species may symbolize four types of Jews. The etrog has taste and smell, and stands for those who possess knowledge and good deeds; the lulav has taste but no smell, representing knowledge but not good deeds; the myrtle, having smell but no taste, portrays those who have good deeds but no knowledge; the willow has neither taste nor smell and represents those with neither good deeds nor knowledge.

Some Jews see the Four Species as symbolizing the human body, with the lulav denoting the spine; the etrog representing the heart; the willow symbolizing the lips; and the myrtle depicting the eyes. Together, they form a shape very similar to a complete person, symbolizing the unity of the Jewish People.

— 61 —

SHEMINI ATZERET: THE ASSEMBLY OF THE EIGHTH DAY

As soon as the Sukkot celebration is complete, there is another holiday in the Jewish cycle. *Shemini Atzeret*, a day dedicated to the spiritual component of the Sukkot festival days, focuses on the relationship between God and the Jews. Shemini Atzeret is the Assembly of the Eighth Day: *shemini* means "eighth," referring to the eighth and final day of Sukkot, and *atzeret* translates as "solemn assembly," or "holding back," suggesting another dimension to Shemini Atzeret. Indeed, the day represents a holding back from ending the festival days of Sukkot. This eighth day, Shemini Atzeret, is dedicated to bringing Sukkot to a state of completion or perfection.

Historically, Shemini Atzeret was the day of sacrifices for the benefit of the People of Israel. Since the Hebrews were primarily farmers in an arid land, a special prayer for rain was made on this day. This prayer remains part of the Shemini Atzeret liturgy.

Since Shemini Atzeret is a festival day in its own right, traditional rituals like lighting candles, reciting the Kiddush over the wine, and saying grace after the meal, are performed at home on the eve of the holiday.

In keeping with the festival's historical significance as a day when God's intervention is sought for a good harvest ahead, a special prayer for rain, called *Geshem*, is still recited, during the Musaf service. While chanting Geshem, the cantor traditionally dons a white gown and chants a melody similar to that for the Days of Awe. Shemini Atzeret is also an appropriate time for reciting the *Yizkor*, the memorial prayer for the dead.

62

SIMCHAT TORAH: COMPLETING THE CYCLE OF READINGS

Several times a week, Jews read a prescribed portion of the Torah, which is divided so that the reading may be completed within a year. *Simchat Torah*, which follows Shemini Atzeret (see number 61), is a joyous holiday that marks the Jews' completing the cycle of Torah readings each year.

Simchat Torah takes place on the second day of Shemini Atzeret. These special days occur on the twenty-second and twenty-third of *Tishri* (the seventh month of the Jewish calendar). However, in Israel, as with all two-day holidays except Rosh Hashanah, Shemini Atzeret is observed for one day and thus includes Simchat Torah.

Known as "Celebration of the Torah" or "Rejoicing of the Torah," Simchat Torah is the day on which the congregation reads the last chapters of Deuteronomy, denoting the completion of the cycle. However, immediately thereafter, the first chapter of Genesis is read to signify the continuing cycle of worship and to demonstrate that the Torah has neither beginning nor end, nor a time when the Jews are not engaged in its reading.

The honor of reading the final verses of the Torah is called *chatan Torah* (the bridegroom of the Torah). The honor of reading Genesis is called *chatan Bereshit* (the bridegroom of Genesis). Should this honor fall upon a woman, the word for "bride" is substituted.

Simchat Torah is primarily celebrated in the synagogue. On the eve of the holiday, when the Ma'ariv service is held, the congregation reads selected verses known as *Ata Horayta* (you have been shown), which recount how God revealed Himself to the Hebrews at Mount Sinai. Upon completion of Ata Horayta, everyone in the synagogue looks toward the ark, and the Torah scrolls are removed.

At this time, every member of the congregation has an opportunity to dance and parade with the Torah scrolls, an act of honor and reverence. (In most non-Orthodox synagogues, this honor also applies to women.) This custom involves seven *hakafot* (revolutions), similar to the hosha-not made during Sukkot. Large congregations add hakafot until every member of the congregation has had the opportunity to march with the Torah scrolls.

The hakafot are performed with one member leading those carrying the Torah scrolls in a circuit around the synagogue. As the Torah scrolls pass, each congregant kisses the scrolls. The rabbi then leads the congregation in reciting special prayers. Once the procession is completed, the next hakafa begins. After services, refreshments may be served, including honey cake and apples. During morning service on the following day, the congregation again performs seven hakafot with the Torah scrolls.

In many congregations, children are invited to join in the hakafot. Some youngsters may carry miniature Torahs while others bear banners or flags with apples placed on the top. Following the processions, the children are often rewarded with treats. Children receive a great deal of attention during the Simchat Torah services because the responsibility of the reading of the Torah will soon fall upon them and the generations to come.

The morning service also has a special *Amidah* (silent recitation) and *Hallel* (psalm of praise). Each member of the congregation (in Orthodox synagogues, each man) is then given an *aliyah*, the blessing before the Torah reading.

The last aliyah, which is reserved for children, is called *kol ha-ne'arim* (translates as "all the boys," though some congregations include girls in this honor). At this time, all the children in the congregation are called up to the *bimah* (the raised platform upon which the Torah scrolls are set when they are read). A large *tallit* (prayer shawl) is spread over the children's heads to form a canopy. Led by an adult, the children recite the blessings over the Torah.

In some congregations, Simchat Torah is also an appropriate time for consecration services. During this time, the congregation welcomes new students to the synagogue's religious school. Generally, the youngsters receive a blessing from the rabbi and perhaps a gift, such as a small prayer book or miniature Torah scroll.

63

HANUKKAH'S RELIGIOUS SIGNIFICANCE

When the Jewish forces recaptured the Temple Mount during the Maccabean Rebellion (see number 5), they wanted to rededicate the Temple. And, in fact, *hanukkah* is the Hebrew word for "dedication." Part of this rededication ceremony required lighting the Temple Menorah, but at the time the Jews could find nothing more than a small quantity of suitable oil, enough to last for one day.

The day after the battle for the Temple Mount, a rider was dispatched to Mount Ephraim, where olive trees grew, to fetch olives to make oil for the Menorah. However, it would have taken three days for the rider to reach his destination and three days to return, not to mention an extra day to press the oil. Although there was no way the oil found in the Temple would have lasted that long, somehow, it did. That small quantity of oil burned for eight days, until the messenger returned with new oil suitable for the Menorah.

Interestingly enough, this episode is not even mentioned in the book of the Maccabees. Instead, the narrative of the miracle of the oil is recounted in the Talmud. While some believe that the miracle was God's work, others feel that it's merely a lovely legend.

According to Jewish tradition, religious leaders, consisting of judges and rabbis who comprised the *Sanhedrin* (the Jewish "Supreme Court"), realized at once that something important had occurred when the Jews reclaimed the Temple Mount, and so they began Hanukkah celebrations the very next year. However, Hanukkah apparently remained a minor holiday. In the Mishna that was compiled several hundred years after the event, there is little reference to Hanukkah, perhaps because it was written at a time when Rome governed Jerusalem and rebellions were not tolerated. This point also supports the contention that the rabbis added the miracle of the oil in the Talmud to emphasize God's involvement and discourage political activism.

Regardless of how the Hanukkah story made its way down through the ages or how much is fact (and it does indeed contain much fact) or legend or even fiction, Hanukkah is imbued with a great deal of meaning on a number of levels.

Clearly, Hanukkah is a religious holiday that celebrates the rededication of the Temple and thanks God with praises, study, and the lighting of the Menorah. Hanukkah commemorates a battle for religious liberty, the freedom to practice Judaism. In fact, numerous scholars, rabbis, and historians have postulated that Hanukkah was the first organized rebellion ever undertaken for the sole sake of religious freedom.

The point is, the Jews strove for the freedom to worship God, and it appears that He helped them in their endeavor. After all, how else could such a tiny, ill-equipped, poorly trained force led by a family of priests overcome the awesome might of the Greek Empire? Then there is the matter of the miracle of the lights. How is it possible for an amount of oil that could scarcely last for one day to keep the Temple Menorah illuminated for eight days? The following reading from Zechariah 4:6 so fittingly reflects this integral Hanukkah motif:

> "Not by might, not by power,
> but by My spirit says the Lord of Hosts."

Some have suggested that the Maccabean Rebellion was motivated by the desire to regain land, but nothing could be further from the truth. It was fought over religious freedom—not over land or political sovereignty. Hanukkah celebrates the miracle of the oil, not the political victory of the Maccabees, who did not regain other land or political independence. The Maccabees belonged to the Hasmonean family of priests. Since priests could not own land, there could have been no land for the Maccabees to reclaim!

It was not until the first century of the Common Era that the Jewish historian Josephus retold the Hanukkah story, which subsequently became popular in the Middle Ages. Indeed, it was Josephus who first referred to Hanukkah as "the feast of lights," as it continues to be known to this day.

64

LIGHTING THE HANUKKAH MENORAH

The most significant rite of Hanukkah is the menorah lighting, a ceremony performed in memory of the Menorah used in the Temple. The Hanukkah menorah, also called *Chanukiah*, has spaces for eight candles all in a row, plus an additional ninth space above the other branches. This last space houses the *shamash* (the "servant" candle). Other types of candelabrum (including electrical ones) are not kosher for this holiday.

Two blessings are recited each night of Hanukkah. An additional blessing, the *Sheheheyanu*, is recited on the first night. On the first night, one candle at the far right of the menorah should be lit. (On each subsequent night, an additional candle is set to the left of the candles lit the previous night.) Then the shamash is lit and used to light the other candles, going from left to right. When all the candles are burning, the shamash is returned to its holder.

If you're wondering why the candles are lit a certain way, you're in good company. A famous debate over this topic occurred between the schools of two esteemed sages, Hillel and Shamai. The House of Shamai proposed that eight candles be lit on the first night, with one removed on each subsequent night, while the House of Hillel believed in just the opposite, saying that as we increase the light, we increase the holiness in the world. As you can see, the House of Hillel prevailed. As to why the candles are lit from left to right—well, it's to honor the newest candle first.

Part of the purpose of lighting the Hanukkah menorah is to publicize the miracle of Hanukkah and share it with the world. Therefore, it is customary for menorahs to be placed in front of a visible window or even set outside the front door. In Israel, some homes are constructed with cutouts in the wall next to the front door for the Hanukkah menorah to be displayed.

Since Hanukkah is eight days long, the holiday encompasses at least one Shabbat. As such, the Hanukkah menorah should never be lit after the Shabbat candles; that would violate the mitzvot of Shabbat (see number 49). In this case, the blessings should be recited first, followed by the lighting of the Hanukkah menorah. Then it's time to light the Shabbat candles.

During Hanukkah, everyone in the home should take part in lighting the menorah, though a married woman may be included in her husband's lighting since they are viewed as an inseparable unit (just as the woman lights Shabbat candles on behalf of the entire family). Ideally, every person in a family has his or her own menorah.

65

HANUKKAH CUSTOMS, TRADITIONS, AND SERVICES

Following the menorah lighting, families sing songs that celebrate the Hanukkah story. Perhaps the most well known of these songs is *Ma'oz Tzur*, or "Rock of Ages" (literally translated as "Mighty Rock").

At this time, children receive Hanukkah *gelt* (a Yiddish term for "money") or candy money. Giving other types of gifts, often one on each night of the festival, is a relatively new tradition practiced by American Jews, a likely reaction to Christmas celebrations, which occur at about the same time of the year.

Popular food dishes cooked during Hanukkah include *latkes* (potato pancakes) and *sufganiot* (jelly doughnuts), both fried in oil as a reminder of the miracle of the oil in the reclaimed Temple, which lasted for eight days.

During Hanukkah, people also play the *dreidel game*, gambling with pennies, candy coins, or other small stakes, and children love to participate. The dreidel is a four-sided spinning top, and each side contains a Hebrew letter:

נ (nun) for *nes*

ג (gimel) for *gadol*

ה (heh) for *hayah*

ש (shin) for *sham*

Together, these four words make up the phrase *nes gadol hayah sham* (a great miracle happened there). In Israel, dreidels substitute the Hebrew letter *p* (*pei*) in place of *shin*, because *pei* denotes *po* (here). There's also another way of looking at these letters: They can stand for the Yiddish words *nit* (nothing), *gantz* (all), *halb* (half), and *shtell* (put), which are the rules of the game and determine what happens to the "pot" after a person spins the dreidel.

According to Kabbalah, however, there is a deeper esoteric meaning to the dreidel letters. The dreidel itself symbolizes Jewish history, and the four letters represent the four empires that tried to destroy the Jews: Babylon, Persia, Greece, and Rome.

Despite its religious implications, Hanukkah is not very high on the list of religious holidays. Most of the observances are conducted in the home, yet Hanukkah does make its presence known in the synagogue.

During morning services, the congregation recites *Hallel* (psalms of praise) and the special *Al Hanisim* (for the miracles) prayer. Torah readings are taken from the book of Numbers (from 7:1–8:4) and relate to the story of rededication. On the Shabbat that falls during Hanukkah, a special Haftorah is read from Zechariah 2:14–4:7. If the festival includes two Shabbats, the second Haftorah is I Kings 7:40–50. Some congregations also add readings from the book of the Maccabees or other works that express Hanukkah themes.

— 66 —

PURIM OBSERVANCES AND CELEBRATIONS

Purim, which commemorates the story of Esther (see numbers 6 and 7), marks the deliverance of the entire Jewish community that lived in Persia 2,500 years ago. It is fitting, therefore, that it be celebrated as a community. Hence, the focus of this holiday lies in the synagogue.

The Sabbath preceding the month of *Adar* is a special Sabbath called *Shabbat Shekalim* (the Shabbath of *shekels*, or money). On this Sabbath, the service includes a special reading of an additional Torah portion dedicated to *tzedakah,* giving to charity (Exodus 30:11–16), and a special Haftorah reading from II Kings 11:17–12:17, which deals with collection of money for repairs to the Temple.

The Sabbath immediately before Purim is called *Shabbat Zachor*, the Sabbath of Remembrance. The Torah portion recounts the Exodus from Egypt and how the Hebrews were attacked by Amalek (Esau's grandson) just after they emerged from the parted Red Sea. The Haftorah for this day, I Samuel 15:1–34, relates how King Saul spared the life of Agag, the sovereign of the nation of Amalek. For this act of mercy, Saul was severely criticized by the Prophet Samuel, who took it upon himself to kill the Amalek king. However, before Samuel took Agag's life, King Agag sired a child, one of whose descendants would turn out to be Haman!

The day before Purim, the thirteenth of Adar (when the Jews fought the hordes determined to exterminate them), the Jews observe the Fast of Esther, which commemorates her three-day fast before walking in unannounced to meet King Ahasuerus. Like all days of fasting, other than Yom Kippur and Tisha B'Av, the fast lasts from dawn until nightfall.

During Purim services, each congregation hears the reading of the book of Esther, commonly referred to as the *Megillah* (scroll). In fact, the book of Esther is one of five megillot that are read on different holidays. The others include the Song of Songs (read on Passover), the book of Ruth (Shavuot), Lamentations (Tisha B'Av), and Ecclesiastes (Sukkot).

This particular Purim text was edited between the fifth and fourth centuries B.C.E. by the Men of the Great Assembly, of which Esther's uncle Mordecai was a member. It is believed the Megillah is largely based on letters written by Mordecai and Esther.

The Megillah is chanted with its own melody. During the reading, it is customary to boo, hiss, or rattle noisemakers each time the reader says the name Haman. The purpose of this practice, called "banging Haman," is to blot out Haman's name.

After the reading of the Megillah, many synagogues organize Purim parades or stage humorous plays called *Purimspiels*. Actually, many people arrive at the synagogue in costume for Purim. Most often, people dress in costumes representing one of the characters in the Purim story, but contemporary political and historical figures appear as well. Anything goes in Purim plays—and the sillier the better! Children enjoy these activities, especially after having sat through the lengthy reading of the Megillah.

While there are several explanations for dressing in disguises or costumes on Purim, the best answer is perhaps that this custom recalls how God saved the Jews while remaining hidden. Dressing in disguises and costumes reminds us how, acting behind the scenes, God delivered the Jews from annihilation.

— *67* —

A TIME FOR REJOICING AND CELEBRATING

In addition to services performed in the synagogue, Jews observe a number of traditions and customs during Purim. The common thread woven through all of them is the emphasis on the celebration of Purim as a day to rejoice and commemorate the deliverance of the Jews from the hands of the king's advisor Haman in Persia. No formal ruling prohibits work on Purim, but Jews do try to take the day off in order to observe the holiday fully.

Although other Jewish holidays carry mitzvot that prohibit eating and other things, on Purim, it is a mitzvah to eat, drink, and be merry. During this celebration, revelers should feel free to imbibe the finest kosher wine or Maccabee beer—while feeling the satisfaction of knowing they are actually carrying out a mitzvah!

Many Jewish holidays boast special and sumptuous foods prepared for a particular historical or symbolic reason, and Purim is no different. A festive meal is appropriate at dinnertime following evening synagogue services, and another one the following day, after the morning service. However, the primary holiday meal is served late in the afternoon after *Mincha* (the afternoon service). At this meal, called the *Purim Seudah*, observant Jews should eat bread and at least one cooked food, drink at least one cup of wine, and dine on anything else they desire.

A traditional treat eaten on Purim is a delightful pastry called *hamen-taschen* (Yiddish for "Haman's pockets") or *oznei Haman* (Hebrew for "Haman's ears"). These pastries are triangular cookies, usually filled with fruit jam or poppy seeds. The three-corner shape of these cookies represents the type of hat Haman is said to have worn, or perhaps his funny-shaped ears.

As mentioned in number 33, *tzedakah* (performing acts of charity and kindness) is an integral part of Judaism. Several tzedakah traditions are practiced specifically during Purim. For instance, a special mitzvah originates from a passage in the Megillah, which quotes Mordecai's declaration that Purim is a time "of feasting and gladness and of sending food to one another, as well as gifts to the poor."

As a result, it is now a Purim tradition to send baskets or packages of food to friends and relatives. These packages are called *mishloach manot* in Hebrew and *shalach-manos* in Yiddish (in both cases, a literal translation is "sending out portions"). These packages may be as simple or as elegant as the sender wishes, but they must contain at least two different types of prepared food ready to be eaten.

Mordecai also instituted the practice of *matanot l'evyonim* (gifts for those in need), which requires making gifts to the poor and donations to charitable organizations. In fact, you should give charity to anyone who asks, with the hope that God will act likewise in responding to your prayers.

— 68 —

RECOGNIZING THE HIDDEN FACE OF GOD
AND THE POWER OF THE INDIVIDUAL

Perhaps the most noteworthy point about the book of Esther is that, unlike any other great Jewish tome, it never mentions God—not even once! As explained in number 6, *esther* shares a root with the Hebrew word for "hidden." Even though God remains hidden in the story of Purim, it is believed that He engineered the story's events. In Hebrew, the "hidden face of God" is called *hester panim*, a concept that Purim celebrates. The lesson of this concept is, although it may appear that humans control their own destinies, God is the architect of all that goes on, controlling events in ways that are not often apparent.

Another way of looking at Purim, not necessarily inconsistent with the notion that God controls events from behind the scenes, is that Purim is a story of survival. It exemplifies the human capacity to change history and events. When Mordecai learns of Haman's plot and the king's decree that would allow the Jews to be slaughtered, he immediately takes action and approaches Esther. Likewise, despite her fears, Esther acts on the situation, and in the end, her actions save her people.

Mordecai and Esther performed boldly. They prayed to God and fasted, but they also took action. Moreover, while the entire Jewish community worshipped and fasted, repenting their previous participation in the festivals that had been forbidden by the rabbis, they fought for their lives and prevailed when the mobs rose against them. Esther, Mordecai, and their fellow Jews serve as models that modern Jews can certainly strive to emulate if and when dire circumstances occur.

— 69 —

What is chametz?

In preparation for Passover, a Jewish home must be rid of all *chametz*. But exactly what is chametz? It's anything that is made from the five major grains (barley, wheat, oats, rye, and spelt) that has not been completely baked within eighteen minutes after coming into contact with water. Further, observant Ashkenazic Jews also avoid rice, corn, peanuts, and beans, since they are commonly used to make bread. Historically, these were often processed alongside wheat, and there was a fear that wheat exposed to water (making it chametz) might have been mixed in.

If you think making a home "chametz-free" is an easy job, think again. It takes days, if not weeks, to accomplish this task. Not only must all chametz be removed from the house, any utensils, dishes, pots, and pans that have come into contact with chametz cannot be used either. This is why some families have an extra set of Passover kitchenware while others use paper products during the holiday.

The entire home, and particularly the kitchen, must be cleaned, scrubbed, and chametz-free. Once everything seems in order, a formal search, called *bedikat chametz*, usually takes place on the night before Passover. Any chametz that is found is carefully set aside, wrapped, and burned the following morning.

Another ritual observed at this time is *mechirat chametz*, the sale of chametz to a Gentile or a rabbi acting with power-of-attorney. In fact, those who sell their chametz intend to repurchase it after Passover. This rite usually takes place when the chametz discovered from the search is burned. It is customary that a renunciation of ownership is declared regarding any chametz that has not been detected.

Once all of the inappropriate foods have been done away with, that leaves the issue of replacing it with the proper items. In addition to buying food that is marked kosher for Passover, Jews need to have a good supply of matzah on hand. Matzah is a grain product made of flour and water, baked quickly so that it does not rise. Enriched matzah, called *matzah ashirah*, contains egg, milk, honey, wine, or fruit juice. It is only permitted on Passover for someone who has difficulty digesting regular matzah.

70

PASSOVER SERVICES AND OBSERVANCES

Today, Passover remains the most widely observed of all the Jewish holidays. Passover's essential message is one of freedom in every connotation

—not only freedom from slavery but also freedom to think, believe, and pray as one chooses.

The Hebrew word for Passover—the holiday that commemorates the sparing of the Hebrews' firstborn sons and their delivery from slavery in Egypt—is *Pesach*, derived from the Hebrew root *peh-samech-chet*, which means "to pass through or over," or "to spare." The holiday has other less commonly employed names as well: *Hag Ha-Aviv* (Holiday of Spring), *Hag Ha-Matzot* (Holiday of Unleavened Bread), and *Z'man Heiruteinu* (Season of Our Liberation).

During the centuries following the Exodus from Egypt (see number 3), the Hebrews were consistent neither in their observance and adherence to the commandments nor in their relationship with God. As a consequence, Passover was sometimes celebrated and sometimes not. After the destruction of the First Temple, the Jews did observe Passover while in exile in Babylon, but without the *paschal offering* (sacrificial lamb). In 516 B.C.E., when some Jews returned to Israel and rebuilt the Temple, the traditional observances at the Temple resumed.

During the era of the Second Temple, Jews once again made pilgrimages to Jerusalem and celebrated the holiday with festive meals, merriment, and study. The Pharisees added to the religious observances by establishing the seder (see numbers 71 and 72) and instituting wine drinking, reclining, and leisurely discussing the narrative. Outside Jerusalem, Passover was observed in the home and at synagogue, and new customs were added to the seder.

After the destruction of the Second Temple, Diaspora Jews developed the *Haggadah*, a book that recounted the story of Passover and included biblical passages, midrashim, poems, and various ceremonies that should be performed during the Passover seder.

Over the years, Passover evolved into a holiday celebrated primarily in the home. Its message of freedom has remained relevant for the Jews in the Diaspora and for people everywhere. Perhaps this is why it is the most widely celebrated Jewish holiday today.

However, synagogue services do play an integral role in the Passover celebration. Three special Sabbaths precede Passover. *Shabbat Parah* occurs two weeks before the month of *Nisan* and on this Shabbat, the Torah portion (Numbers 19:1–22) explains the purification process involving the sacrifice of the *Parah Adumah* (red cow).

The Sabbath immediately preceding Nisan is *Shabbat Ha-Chodesh*. The Torah portion read that day (Exodus 12:1–20) recounts the commandments of the Passover sacrifice and preparations for departing from Egypt. The third Sabbath, just before Passover, is called *Shabbat Ha-Gadol* (the Great Sabbath). The Haftorah read on this Shabbat (Malachi 3:4–24) refers to the final redemption of the Messianic Age that will be ushered in by Elijah: "Behold, I will send you Elijah the prophet. Before the coming of the great and terrible day of the Lord."

An additional observance preceding Pesach applies to a particular category of Jews. On the day just before Passover, there is the Fast of the Firstborn, when all firstborn males commemorate the fact that while their Egyptian counterparts were slaughtered, God spared the firstborn Jewish males. Should this day occur on Sabbath, the fast is made on Thursday.

The first day of Passover is *Yom Tov* (the Good Day). During this day (two days for the Orthodox outside of Israel), work, travel, and other everyday activities are not permitted.

Readings during the eight days of Passover are from all parts of the Torah because of the numerous times the Exodus and Passover narrative are mentioned. Torah portions are read from Exodus (first, third, fourth, fifth, and seventh days), Leviticus (second day), Numbers (sixth day), and Deuteronomy (eighth day).

Liturgy services during Passover are similar to those for other festivals but with a few distinctive features. During the Musaf service on the first day, congregations recite a special prayer for the dew called *Tfilat Tal*. This prayer is the counterpart to Geshem, the prayer for rain that is made on Shemini Atzeret (see number 61). On the last day of Passover, the liturgy also includes *Yizkor* (memorial service).

—— 71 ——

THE PASSOVER SEDER

During the periods of the First and Second Temples, Passover centered on pilgrimages to Jerusalem, where each family was required to sacrifice a paschal lamb at the Temple. After the destruction of the Second Temple and the dispersal of the Jews, the focus shifted to the synagogue and even more to the home. Today, the injunction to remember and to tell the Passover story is carried out primarily in the home at a function called the seder.

The seder includes a special meal and related ceremonies that are celebrated on the first night of Passover. (Many Diaspora Jews also hold a seder on the second night). The word *seder* is Hebrew for "order," or "order of the service," so the order and specifics of the seder ceremonies hold great importance.

Conducting a seder is not as hard as you might think. All you have to do is follow the *Haggadah*, a book that contains the order of the seder. The title *Haggadah* comes from the Hebrew *l'hagid* ("to tell"), and the Haggadah is the telling of the Exodus story that is central to the Passover celebration.

It is likely that the first Haggadah was published in the eleventh century; the first illustrated Haggadah appeared in 1482 in Spain. Since then, the Haggadah has been published in thousands of editions. Today, Haggadot come in a wide variety of traditional, secular, feminist, mystical, and vegetarian versions. Some families have even produced their own Haggadot.

There is plenty of advance preparation for a seder, and in order to follow the Haggadah the seder table must first be set. The objects present on the seder table are highly symbolic and play a ceremonial role in the dinner. Here's what a seder table should include:

- A special matzah cover with dividers for three pieces of matzah
- Cushioned chairs or pillows on each chair so that everyone can

       recline and be comfortable during the seder (a symbol of freedom and wealth)

- Sufficient kosher red wine and/or grape juice (enough for four cups per person)
- Napkin or doily to cover the middle piece of matzah (the *afikoman*, a piece of matzah set aside and later hidden for the children)
- A Kiddush cup for everyone, and one special goblet to serve as the cup of Elijah
- A pitcher and bowl for washing hands
- At least one bowl filled with salt water that will be needed for dipping
- One Haggadah per person (preferably uniform)
- A seder plate (the contents of the seder plate will be discussed in further detail)
- Flowers (always appropriate but not required)

The seder plate, or *ke'arah*, contains the five symbols of the seder. While any dish can be used, some families use a special seder plate for Passover. Five specific food dishes appear on the seder plate:

- *Karpas*, a green vegetable (usually parsley, watercress, or celery), symbolizes the greenness of spring. During the seder, the karpas is dipped into the salt water.
- *Maror*, bitter herbs or horseradish, is a dish that represents the bitterness of slavery.

- *Charoset*, a mixture of chopped nuts, apples, wine, and cinnamon, is reminiscent of the mortar used by the Hebrew slaves when they toiled in Egypt.
- *Beitzah*, a roasted (hardboiled) egg, symbolizes the continuity of life and the commencement of spring.
- *Zeroa*, a roasted shankbone, represents the sacrifice of the paschal lamb.

Beyond the symbolic foods described above, Jewish families prepare a variety of special dishes for the Passover seder, all of which should be kosher. Ashkenazic Jews generally eat a traditional meal of gefilte fish and matzah ball soup, followed by roast chicken, turkey, or brisket of beef.

—— 72 ——

KEY ELEMENTS OF THE SEDER CEREMONY

After lighting holiday candles, the seder begins with the blessing over the first cup of wine. A total of four cups of wine are poured during the Passover seder, representing the four promises God made to the Hebrews: that He will free them from the burdens of bondage, deliver them from slavery, redeem them with an outstretched arm, and take them to be "My people" (Exodus 6:6–8).

After drinking the first cup of wine, a second round is poured, and then it's time for everyone to wash their hands in preparation for dipping the karpas in salt water. (As mentioned in the previous point, the karpas is eaten as a symbol of the tears shed by the Hebrew slaves in Egypt.)

Next comes *yahatz*, a ceremony that requires breaking a piece of the matzah (the middle piece from the special three-layered matzah covering). After the matzah is broken in half, the larger piece becomes the *afikoman*, a piece hidden from the children present at the seder. Before the end of the seder, the children will search for it.

At this point, it is time to relate the Passover narrative, which begins with the youngest child present at the table asking the Four Questions. During the course of the narration, as the gathered recite the ten plagues, each person spills ten drops of wine from their cup (usually either by pouring or dipping their finger into the wine). This custom serves as a reminder that when other people suffer, our joy is diminished. The seder participants then drink the second cup of wine and a blessing is made.

Again, everyone washes their hands, this time while reciting a blessing. A motzi is made over the matzah and a second blessing is said for the specific mitzvah of eating matzah. Then, each person dips the *maror* (bitter herbs) in the *charoset* (the mixture of apples, cinnamon, wine, and chopped nuts).

After the meal, the children search for the afikoman. Usually, when the children find it, they receive gifts as a ransom to allow the seder to continue. (An alternative custom is for the children to hide the afikoman for their parents to find.) At this point, everyone eats a piece of the afikoman and the seder proceeds with the after-meal grace and the drinking of the third cup of wine. As the final cup of wine is poured for each guest, a special cup is filled for the prophet Elijah. The door is opened to welcome Elijah, and a blessing praising God is made over the wine, which is then consumed.

The final part of the *Haggadah* (the book that retells the Exodus story) contains songs and praises to God, and the remainder of *Hallel* (Psalms 113–118) is recited. The seder is concluded with a poem and song, ending with the words *Le shana ha-ba'ah b'Yerushalayim* (next year in Jerusalem).

73

SHAVUOT: THE FESTIVAL OF WEEKS

The holiday *Shavuot* is known by many names: *Hag Habikkurim* (the Festival of the First Fruits), *Hag Matan Torateinu* (the Festival of the Giving of Our Torah), and *Hag Hakatzir* (the Feast of the Harvest). Because Shavuot falls on the fiftieth day from the second day of Passover, it is sometimes known as Pentecost (a Greek term that has become famous thanks to its importance in Christianity).

In Hebrew, *shavuot* means "weeks," which is why Shavuot is also known as the Festival of Weeks. In fact, Shavuot occurs exactly seven weeks after the second day of Passover, a time period that represents the interval when the Hebrews left Egypt but had not yet received the Torah.

Shavuot commemorates the day when according to Jewish tradition,

God revealed the entire Torah to Moses on Mount Sinai. That is why the period between Passover and Shavuot is a time of solemnity. During certain segments of this period, tradition forbids marriage ceremonies and playing of live music. The devout avoid cutting their hair, for this is a season for preparing oneself to receive the Torah, a time for study and meditation.

Just like Passover and Sukkot, the other two pilgrimage festivals when Jews traveled to Jerusalem to celebrate and give thanks at the Temple, Shavuot is laden with both historical and agricultural importance. Unlike those other two festivals, however, Shavuot is not a lengthy holiday: It lasts for only one day (or two days, in the case of more traditional Diaspora Jews).

Despite its religious significance, the Torah itself first mentions Shavuot as an agricultural festival marking the transition between the barley harvest and the start of the wheat-ripening season. Before the destruction of the Temple, Jews used this brief respite from work to travel to Jerusalem, to celebrate and offer sacrifices at the Temple. After the destruction of the First Temple, many pilgrims continued to come from Babylon. Communities that could not send all their members dispatched a representative delegation. After the razing of the Second Temple in 70 C.E., pilgrimages became impossible. Hence, the focus of the holiday shifted from its dual agricultural and spiritual importance to emphasize the spiritual aspect.

Like all Jewish holidays, Shavuot begins the night before. At home, Jews conduct the customary candle-lighting ceremony and blessings, making Kiddush over wine or grape juice and the blessing over the bread (usually two loaves), before enjoying a festive holiday meal.

Tradition holds that Jews should have at least one dairy meal during Shavuot. One explanation is that it serves as a reminder of God's promise to deliver the Hebrews into a land flowing with milk and honey (Exodus 3:8). Another explanation suggests that when the Hebrews received the Torah (which includes the dietary laws), they did not yet have separate meat and dairy dishes and thus had to eat only dairy until they could have proper utensils. A more symbolic explanation is that Jews eat dairy because the Hebrews were as innocent as newborns, whose only food is milk.

It is common practice on Shavuot to decorate both the home and synagogue with flowers, plants, and tree branches, perhaps because foliage is reminiscent of Mount Sinai, which was forested and lush with greens. Plants also serve as a reminder that Pharaoh's daughter found Moses among reeds in the Nile.

Perhaps the most important Shavuot tradition has to do with the custom of staying awake most of, or even all of, the night to study the Torah. This practice is called *Tikkun Leil Shavuot*. The word *tikkun* comes from the verb *letakein* ("to fix or rectify"). A Midrashic interpretation suggests that the reason for this ancient practice of staying awake all night studying on Shavuot is to symbolically "rectify" the fact that the Hebrews overslept on Shavuot morning.

This tradition began sometime in the sixteenth century in Safed, Israel, a Kabbalistic center. Today, people frequently gather to study in the synagogue, but the synagogue need not be the only location to do so.

74

SHAVUOT SERVICES

During Shavuot, the holiday that commemorates the Hebrews receiving the Torah, morning Torah readings include the revelation at Mount Sinai and the giving of the Ten Statements (Exodus 19:1–20:23). The portion involving the Ten Statements is recited in a special chant.

In many Ashkenazic synagogues, the Shavuot service includes a liturgical poem titled *"Akdamot Milin."* Written in Aramaic by Rabbi Meir ben Isaac of Worms, Germany, in the eleventh century, this poem exalts Israel's attachment to the Torah and describes what conditions will be like during the time of the Messiah. Sephardic congregations recite a *piyyut* (religious poem) called *azharut*, which lists the 613 mitzvot. *Yizkor*, the memorial service, is recited on the first day or on the second day for those who observe two days.

On Shavuot, congregations also read from the book of Ruth, which relates the inspiring story of a Moabite woman who, after the death of her Jewish husband and her father-in-law, voluntarily chose Judaism in order to be with her mother-in-law. Most likely, you've heard some version of Ruth's famous unselfish pledge to her mother-in-law: "For wherever you go, I will go; wherever you lodge, I will lodge; your people will be my people and your God my God" (Ruth 1:16).

The saga of Ruth is recounted on Shavuot for two reasons. First, part of the story happened during the barley and wheat harvests. Second, like the Hebrews at the foot of Mount Sinai, Ruth freely accepted the Torah and Judaism, making her the first recorded convert to this faith. What is more, Ruth became the great-grandmother of King David.

The concept of being given the Torah and opting to embrace it remains relevant today because, as a midrash explains, the Sinai experience touches all Jews since all Jews—past, present, and future—were present at Sinai.

Since Shavuot marks the giving of the Torah, many Reform, Reconstructionist, and Conservative congregations hold confirmation services on Shavuot (see number 73). Confirmation is an occasion that recognizes the completion of a course of study for those who continue on, past bar mitzvah and bat mitzvah, to several more years of Jewish education.

75

TISHA B'AV: MEMORIALIZING
THE DESTRUCTION OF THE TEMPLES

Most revealing about *Tisha B'Av* is its name. It is simply a date: the ninth day of the month of Av. This day is consecrated not because it is a harvest festival or because it commemorates a major triumph in Jewish history. Rather, it is a date memorializing a great tragedy for the Jewish people—the destruction of the Temples.

According to the Jewish tradition, both the First and the Second

Temples were destroyed on the same date—the ninth of Av. The Babylonians laid the First Temple in ruins in 586 B.C.E., and the Romans destroyed the Second Temple in 70 C.E. The destruction of the Second Temple commenced the Diaspora, which lasted until the establishment of the modern State of Israel in 1948.

But the destruction of the Second Temple was not the last tragedy to occur on Tisha B'Av. On this day in 1290, King Edward ordered the expulsion of the Jews from England. Two hundred and two years later, in 1492, the Jews were expelled from Spain. For all of these reasons, Tisha B'Av has come to represent a day when it is appropriate to mourn the afflictions that have befallen Jews over the centuries.

Given its plaintive nature, it's not surprising that Tisha B'Av is a day of fasting. With the exception of Yom Kippur, this is the only fast day that lasts from sundown to sundown. (All the other days of fasting begin in the morning and end at night.)

Tisha B'Av marks the culmination of a three-week period of mourning that began with the fast of the seventeenth day of *Tammuz* (commemorating the first breach of the walls enclosing Jerusalem). This period has restrictions: weddings and parties are not permitted, and people do not cut their hair or wear new clothing. From the first through the ninth of Av (except on Shabbat), observant Jews also abstain from meat and wine.

The restrictions on Tisha B'Av are similar to those on Yom Kippur (see numbers 55, 56, and 57), but also incorporate certain practices associated with mourning. On this day, Jews must avoid the following:

- Eating or drinking
- Washing or bathing (though individuals may wash fingers up to the knuckles)
- Shaving or wearing cosmetics and lotions
- Wearing leather shoes
- Having sexual relations
- Working (at least until noon) or doing any pleasurable activity
- Smiling, laughing, having idle conversations, or greeting others
- Sitting on regular chairs (instead, people are instructed to sit on a low stool or on the ground)
- Studying the Torah (with the exception of certain subjects related to mourning, since the study of Torah is a joyful experience)

If Tisha B'Av falls on a Saturday, Shabbat takes precedence. Therefore, the fast is postponed until Saturday night through sundown on Sunday. In such an event, Jews need not eliminate bathing altogether and may do so the following day (though not the following night).

On this day, following the typical evening Ma'ariv service, congregations read from the book of Lamentations, where the prophet Jeremiah describes the destruction of the First Temple. Following Lamentations, congregants recite prayers of mourning.

To emphasize the unique nature of this day of mourning, it is customary to remove the curtain from the Holy Ark where the Torahs are kept and to drape the ark in black. In some synagogues, the main lights are turned off and prayers are recited by candlelight. On the morning of Tisha B'Av, at Shacharit prayers, men do not wear tallit and tefillin. While small tzitzit are donned, no blessing is made.

By fasting, carrying out traditional mourning rituals, and attending prayer services customized to reflect the day's gravity, Jews create the proper milieu for remembering some infamous points in Jewish history. In this fashion, present-day Jews strengthen their links with the Jews of the past.

— 76 —

TU B'SHEVAT: NEW YEAR FOR TREES

Like Tisha B'Av, the Jewish occasion that commemorates the destruction of the Temples (see number 75), the name of the holiday *Tu B'Shevat* denotes the date on which it falls—the fifteenth day of the month of Shevat. Tisha B'Av is also known as *Rosh Hashanah L'Ilanot* (New Year for Trees), which is exactly what this holiday is about.

Leviticus 19:23–25 states that the fruit from trees may not be eaten during the first three years. The fruit of the fourth year belongs to God, but after the fourth year, the fruit may be eaten. The purpose of Tu B'Shevat is to calculate the age of trees for tithing, because it is the boundary date for determining the age of trees. This date was probably selected to mark the end of the rain season in ancient Israel.

On a more spiritual level, Tu B'Shevat is a time for prayer and judgment regarding trees. The premise is that, whenever one of God's creatures begins to grow, God contemplates its future. Therefore, it is proper to pray on behalf of that creature—animate or inanimate.

The best way to celebrate Tu B'Shevat is by planting a tree. This is a prevalent practice in Israel, where trees play an important ecological role, reclaiming the desert and providing shade in an arid, sandy terrain.

Eating fruits, particularly those native to Israel, such as grapes, figs, pomegranates, olives, and dates, is another common custom during this holiday. Some Jews make these fruits the center of a special meal or even a Tu B'Shevat seder, with recitations, songs, and wine. In fact, having a seder on Tu B'Shevat is fast becoming a new tradition in many Jewish communities.

With the founding of Israel, it became a common custom for Jewish children in other countries to collect funds to be sent to Israel for the planting of trees and the establishment of forests. Although not as widespread as some others, this tradition continues today.

Part 5

CEREMONIES AND MILESTONES

JUDAISM ATTACHES GREAT IMPORTANCE TO HUMAN LIFE. As such, this religion has evolved to include a variety of traditions and ceremonies that mark important milestones in a Jewish individual's life. All societies have practices and rituals that address life's big picture existential themes: growing up, getting married, having children, growing old, dying, and moving on to the world beyond our earthly existence.

What does life mean, and how do we make sense of it? These are questions human beings have been pondering for ages, and marking important rites of passage throughout life is an integral part of synthesizing the human experience. Like any other tradition, Judaism has ceremonies that recognize a young person's growth into adulthood, celebrate a couple's lifetime commitment through marriage, and honor and remember those who have died.

From celebrating the birth of a new child, to mourning the passing of a loved one, Judaism offers room for acknowledging and expressing joy, grief, and everything in between.

77

FINDING A SOUL MATE THROUGH A MATCHMAKER

In any society, marriage is one of life's most significant milestones, and the prospect of finding a soul mate is integral to the Jewish culture. But exactly how do Jewish individuals believe you go about finding a soul mate? One view holds that there is really nothing special to do—once an individual gets married, the other person is ipso facto his or her soul mate. According to one midrashic story, marriages are arranged in heaven and, in fact, ever since creating the world in six days, God has been busy arranging matches!

When it comes to matters of the heart, a person can grow impatient awaiting "true love." Sometimes, you must take matters into your own hands, either on behalf of yourself or for someone else.

The *Mishna* (code of Jewish law) describes festivities that occurred in Jerusalem on the fifteenth day of Av and on the afternoon of Yom Kippur. On these occasions, single women dressed in white and danced in the vineyards, hoping to be chosen as a bride by one of the attentive men. However, such activities were not always successful, and young women (or their parents) would grow weary waiting for "fate" to step in. And so, the business of arranging marriages arose.

For many centuries, the task of finding suitable marriage partners was left to a *shadchan* (marriage broker, or matchmaker), who would arrange a *shidukh*, the Hebrew word for "marital match." The Aramaic version of this word is *sheket*, which also means "quiet." That is, the term *shidukh* reflects tranquillity or peacefulness—the idea is that the match should prove serene and happy for all concerned and also bring some relief to the matched individual's parents!

The "profession" of a shadchan became very popular in the thirteenth and fourteenth centuries but this popularity waned as the notion of romantic love gained the upper hand when it came to choosing marriage partners. However, matchmakers—even though they weren't always the brightest or most scrupulous people—remained important, particularly in the *shtetls* (small Jewish villages) of Eastern Europe, up until the nineteenth century.

In contemporary society, however, the use of matchmakers is rare and is generally limited to more observant Jewish families. These days, there are other proactive (and sometimes high-tech) paths folks can take to find a soul mate—like cyber dating, for starters.

— 78 —

THE JEWISH VIEW OF MARRIAGE

The Jewish tradition views marriage as the ideal state. In fact, the Hebrew word for the first part of the marriage ceremony is *kiddushin*—"holiness," or "sanctification." (See the following point for more on the kiddushin.) In the Jewish culture, marriage is sacred for two reasons. First, it fulfills the important mitzvah to procreate. Second, the physical union of husband and wife is considered sacred, in and of itself, because two beings become one.

The basis for this second point is rooted in the Torah. According to the book of Genesis, God created man and woman as one being. Later, God removed Adam's rib to fashion woman as a separate person. Consequently, Judaism holds the union of a man and a woman in marriage to be a consecrated event that rejoins two souls, two separate beings, who again become one whole.

The Hebrew word for "soul mate" is *zivug*, and this term illustrates how Judaism views each married couple—as soul mates. Although this idea is popular in contemporary culture, it has been well established in Judaism since the narrative of Adam and Eve.

According to the Talmud, when God created Adam, Adam had two faces. When God split him in two, one became Eve. God brought Eve to Adam and they were reunited. Therefore, the joining of man and woman is the reunification of a sundered soul. It is also written in the Talmud that forty days before a male child is conceived, it is announced in heaven whose daughter he will marry. This perfect match is called *bashert* ("fate" or "destiny" in Yiddish).

Consequently, Judaism treats marriage as the means by which two human beings unite and reach a complete state that brings them closer to God. While the man and the woman retain their distinct identities, each one can become truly whole only when united with their significant other.

Because the union of husband and wife is sanctified, the married couple has the opportunity and responsibility to make their home into a miniature sanctuary, or *mikdat me'at*. Thus, the home and the raising of children are central to Judaism, and the home plays a prominent role in the celebrating holidays and festivals.

—— 79 ——

MITZVOT THAT DEAL WITH MARRIAGE AND SEXUAL RELATIONS

In the Jewish tradition, there are many mitzvot associated with marriage. More than likely you are acquainted with God's commandment to "be fruitful and multiply" (Genesis 1:28). In Judaism, to marry and have children is not considered an option. It is a mitzvah, and it is stated as a requirement in the *Shulchan Aruch*, the Code of Jewish Law. In order to fulfill this commandment, each couple must have at least one male and one female child.

The importance placed upon procreation is also emphasized in the Talmud, where it is written that, when each person enters the world to come, he or she will have to answer the following three questions: Were you honest in your business dealings? Did you have a set time for Torah study? Did you raise a family?

Recall the story of Jacob, who entered Egypt with a band of seventy adults. A little more than two centuries later, the Hebrews emerged from

Egypt some two to three million strong. While these numbers might seem astronomical at first, if you do the math you'll see that if the Hebrews obeyed this mitzvah, the population that came forth from Egypt is well within the realm of the probable.

But there are more marriage-related mitzvot beyond those that have to do with procreation. The verb "to know" is used in the Bible to represent sexual relations. The use of this word reflects Judaism's emphasis on the unity of the heart and mind with the physical body that occurs in sexual intimacy. Although Judaism assigns purely libidinous desire to the realm of "evil" impulses, it also recognizes the importance of sexuality, which can be a beautiful, meaningful, and even holy act. Hence, the mitzvot that deal with sex are both positive and negative.

There are two major objectives behind Halakah concerning sex. First, as alluded to above, the sexual act is seen as an opportunity to achieve spiritual unity and create a "holy" encounter. It is meant to add a deeper dimension to the marital relationship. The other main objective of sex is procreation, so that Jews observe God's mandate to "be fruitful and multiply." Consequently, any sexual act that results in the destruction of semen, such as ejaculation outside the vagina, is forbidden.

This law may explain why sexual acts between men are forbidden, but an interdiction on sexual relations between women is absent. (This does not mean that Judaism condones lesbianism.) It may also account for why homosexual desires do not violate Halakah. It is only the sexual act itself that is prohibited. Masturbation is likewise enjoined, for the obvious reason that it allows for the "spilling of seed."

A lesser-known area regarding the mitzvot that govern sex has to do with the law of *niddah* (separation). According to this law, men may not have sexual relations when their wives are menstruating and must further wait a minimum of seven days after there is no sign of bleeding. As soon as possible after the seventh "clean day," the woman is to immerse herself in a *mikvah* (a ritual pool). Thereafter, sexual relations should be resumed.

Because of this law, a husband and wife may not have sexual relations for at least twelve days out of each month. It has been suggested that the law of niddah improves the quality of sex, by limiting the time in which husband and wife may engage in intimate relations. Furthermore, a period of abstinence each month may increase male fertility.

Given the value placed upon human life and the mitzvah to procreate, birth control and abortion are acceptable only in limited circumstances. Generally, both are permitted when the mother's life is in jeopardy. With advances in methods of contraception, Judaism has, in some cases, adopted a more liberal stance in the area of birth control. While a condom is not allowed because it destroys the "seed," the birth control pill is permissible. This is a perfect example of how mitzvot must continually be interpreted when new situations and conditions arise.

80

KIDDUSHIN AND THE KETUBAH:
BETROTHAL AND MARRIAGE CONTRACT

Once an individual finds his or her soul mate, or *bashert*, certain conditions must be met before a Jewish marriage ceremony can take place. The couple must undergo the engagement or betrothal period, known as the *kiddushin*. Derived from the Hebrew root *kodesh*, meaning "holy," this term reflects the idea that the man and woman have become consecrated to each other. In recent times kiddushin has merged into the marriage ritual and is held during the first part of the wedding ceremony.

Kiddushin requires that in order for a woman to be acquired and a marriage made, one of the following three conditions must be satisfied (although, ordinarily, all three are fulfilled):

1. Payment of money or something of value
2. A written contract
3. Physical consummation of the relationship

The notion that a woman is "acquired" is no doubt troublesome to our modern way of thinking. However, Jewish tradition does stipulate that regardless of who proposed the match or what the parents may demand, a woman may be "acquired" only with her consent. In fact, the written marital contract is designed, for the most part, to protect the woman.

Today, the thing of value customarily offered is the wedding ring. Jewish wedding bands are not supposed to be jeweled—a practice that arose to avoid the possibility of acquiring a wife by fraud. Only an expert can discern the value of gems, but anyone can see the worth of an unadorned ring.

Further, the wedding ring is not supposed to have substantial monetary value, since its purpose has nothing to do with buying or selling a woman. Rather, the woman's approval of this object of value serves to indicate her acceptance of her future husband.

If there is to be a double ring ceremony, which is not required in Judaism, it is also advisable for the bride to have a plain wedding band for the groom.

In addition to betrothal ceremonies, a couple must also sign the marriage contract (different from the betrothal contract previously mentioned). The marriage contract is called a *ketubah*, a term that comes from the Hebrew word *katav* (writing).

Ketubot range from standard printed certificates with blanks filled in, to beautiful customized works of calligraphy and decorated pieces of art that may be framed and displayed in the home. The text may be written in the traditional Aramaic or include modern expressions.

The ketubah is designed to protect the woman in marriage. It delineates the obligations and responsibilities a husband has toward the wife in terms of helping her to raise the children, accepting financial responsibility in the event of divorce and stipulating conditions of inheritance upon the death of the husband. By mutual agreement, additional provisions may be made to the contract.

81

Key elements in a Jewish wedding ceremony

Jewish weddings vary widely, depending on the couple's religious denomination, cultural traditions, and personal preferences—there is really no single way to celebrate a Jewish wedding. However, it is possible to discuss the traditional Jewish wedding ceremony that precedes the party.

Not all of these customs and observances are performed at every Jewish wedding. Often, couples prefer to have a personal hand in determining their ceremony, sometimes foregoing certain rituals and in other places embellishing the litany with original and personal thoughts. (Bear in mind that interfaith ceremonies are a separate issue; for more information, refer to number 34.)

In the basic ceremony conducted in accordance with the principles of Judaism, custom dictates that the bride (*kalah* or *kallah*) and groom (*chatan*) are not allowed to see each other for one week prior to the wedding. Generally, on the Shabbat preceding the wedding, an *aliyah* (the honor of reading from the Torah or reciting a blessing over the Torah reading that is held during services) is given to the groom or to the couple. This special aliyah is called an *aufruf.* The congregation blesses the couple and, in some synagogues, showers the couple with candy. In other synagogues, in lieu of an aliyah, the couple is called to the *bimah* (the raised platform upon which the Torah scrolls are set when read) for a prenuptial blessing.

On the day of their wedding, the bride and groom are expected to fast. By fasting, repenting their sins, and being forgiven in the process, the new couple commences their life together with a clean slate.

Before the ceremony, the bride is veiled in remembrance of Rebecca, who veiled her face when she was brought to Isaac to be his wife. In more traditional circles, it is common for the groom to wear a long white kittel similar to that worn on Yom Kippur and Passover.

Jewish wedding ceremonies can take place anywhere, and a wedding held in a synagogue is no more sanctified than one held in a hotel ballroom, in a home, or outdoors. What is required is that during the ceremony the couple be standing under the *chupah* ("chamber" or "covering" in Hebrew), a wedding canopy that is the central symbol of the ceremony. The chupah can be made of a tallit supported by four poles, of fine fabric such as silk, or of even a floral arrangement. Sometimes, the chupah is embroidered with a biblical quotation.

The chupah is symbolic of several things. Foremost, it depicts the roof of the new home, in which the bride and groom will live and raise their family. Second, the chupah suggests a royal canopy, for tradition holds that on the wedding day, the bride and groom are like a king and queen. The chupah also represents a third element of creating a marriage (sexual relations).

With the chupah in place, the wedding ceremony can begin. The first part of the ceremony is known as *kiddushin* or "sanctified." Historically, the kiddushin might have occurred as much as one year before the *nisuin* (full-fledged marriage), but today they form two parts of the same event.

First, the wedding party comes to stand under the chupah. Sometimes, the bride is led to the chupah by her mother and mother-in-law or by any two women, and the groom is ushered by his father and father-in-law or by any two men. At other times, both sets of parents escort their respective children. In this case, the groom arrives to the chupah first and awaits the bride.

In Judaism, there is no such concept as "giving away" the bride. That is why the bride is escorted by two people and not just by her father. The bride's parents remain with her under the chupah during the ceremony, as do the groom's parents.

Jewish law does not require the presence of a rabbi at the wedding ceremony. In fact, it is incorrect to say that the rabbi "marries" the couple. In Judaism, two witnesses are sufficient; the rabbi's presence only helps to ensure that the ceremony is properly performed. It is true, however, that a rabbi or public official must officiate the wedding in order to comply with modern civil law.

When the bride reaches the chupah, she is led seven times around the groom for several reasons. The Kabbalah, for instance, suggests that the bride symbolizes the earth; by encircling the groom seven times, she reenacts the seven days of Creation. This is particularly significant since the married couple will soon become involved in the creation of new lives.

Blessings over the wine follow. First the rabbi drinks from the wine, and then the groom and the bride do likewise. The groom places the ring on the bride's right index finger, reciting, "You are hereby sanctified to me with this ring according to the Laws of Moses and Israel." This act of sanctification is kiddushin. If there is a double ring ceremony, the bride makes a similar vow. At this point, kiddushin is complete.

Next, the ceremony proceeds with the reading of the ketubah, which serves to separate the two parts of the service. Then, the ceremony continues with *nisuin* ("elevation"). Seven blessings are recited, the first of which is the blessing over the wine. Again, the rabbi drinks from the goblet, and the groom and the bride follow.

The ceremony concludes with the glass breaking, probably the best-known feature of a Jewish wedding. A glass is wrapped in a cloth, and then the groom smashes it with his right foot. This action reminds the Jews that even on the happiest of occasions, they must remember the destruction of the Temple. This custom also reminds the gathered that the world is broken and they must help repair it. Another rationale suggests that the love between bride and groom will last until the scattered shards of glass come back together.

Then new husband and wife are escorted to a private room, where they are secluded for a brief time. This custom, known as *yichud*, is symbolic of the husband bringing his wife to his home. Although they are left alone and no one knows what does or does not go on inside, the couple is not expected to actually consummate the marriage at that time.

As with any joyous event, it is customary to celebrate the wedding with music, dancing, and fine food. However, this is not the focal point of the wedding day. The center of attention should be the ceremony where the bride and groom are joined as soul mates.

82

MARKING THE BIRTH OF A NEW CHILD

There is a Jewish adage that "with each child, the world begins anew." Indeed, what event could be more wondrous, beautiful, and sacred than the arrival of a new life into this world? When such an occasion presents itself, the Jewish people have much to celebrate.

According to Judaism, a child's soul exists prior to his or her birth, but life begins at the time of birth—more specifically, when the child is halfway emerged from the womb. The new soul that enters the world is considered pure and chaste. The concept of original sin is foreign to Judaism. Of course, the Jews recognize that people commit sins as the years go by, but they believe that humans begin their lives with a clean slate.

After the birth of a child, the father is given an *aliyah* (the honor of making a blessing over the Torah). A blessing is recited at that time for the health of the new mother and baby. This may also be an occasion when a baby girl is named.

In the Jewish tradition, the naming of a new child is very important, since the name a person bears reflects that person's basic nature. Ashkenazic Jews name their children in remembrance of a recently deceased relative. This tradition honors the memory of the departed but also follows a superstition that a child should not be named after someone who is living.

On the other hand, Sephardic Jews name their children after living relatives. They generally don't name a son after the father or a daughter after the mother, but it's perfectly proper to name a child after a grandparent.

Although no formal Jewish commandment specifies that a child must have a Hebrew name, most Jewish parents give their child a Hebrew middle name. The child uses the Hebrew name during important occasions and ceremonies, such as being called to the Torah for an aliyah or identifying the bride and groom in the ketubah.

A child's formal Hebrew name comes with the word *ben* (son of) or *bat* (daughter of) and the father's name (though some non-Orthodox families may include the mother's name). For instance, Shmuel ben Yosef is the full name of Samuel, the son of Joseph. If the child is a kohein, the title *ha-Kohein* is added; if the child is a Levite, the title *Ha-Levi* will follow.

83

THE JEWISH VIEW ON ADOPTION AND ABORTION

As already discussed, in Judaism, it is a mitzvah to get married and have children. But what happens if a married couple wants to have children, but they are physically unable to do so? The commandment to "be fruitful and multiply" may be satisfied by adopting a child. Jewish law does not directly address the matter of adoption, nor is there a formal adoption ceremony. However, several beautiful prayers and blessings have been written for this special occasion.

If a Jewish couple adopts a child born of a Gentile mother, the child must undergo the conversion process. Not surprisingly, the conversion procedure for a child is not as rigorous as that for an adult. Although the process does vary according to the branch of Judaism to which the family adheres, it generally includes the following:

- Approval by a rabbinic court
- Circumcision performed with appropriate ceremony
- Immersion of the child in a *mikvah* (ritual bath)
- A commitment the child will receive a Jewish education

However, many Reform rabbis will forego this conversion requirement so long as the child is raised as a Jew and given a Jewish education.

In most respects, all obligations parents have toward their natural children apply to adoptive children and vice versa concerning the child toward the parents. An adopted child becomes a part of the Jewish community and is welcomed like all Jewish children with a *bris* (circumcision ceremony), a *Pidyon Ha-Ben* redemption ceremony for the firstborn son, if applicable, and a naming ceremony. (See numbers 84 and 85.)

As for abortion, Judaism takes a unique position on this very sensitive issue. Unlike some other religions that completely ban abortion under any circumstances, Judaism has always allowed abortions—has even required abortions—to preserve a life. This book has already stressed that Judaism holds each and every life to be sacred. As such, when the life of a woman is in jeopardy, it is clear that the pregnancy must be terminated.

However, when it comes to this controversial topic, there is no unanimity among the respective movements of Judaism beyond this clear maxim. The traditional point of view is that abortion is not permitted other than when the woman's life is in danger. But what about cases where a woman's health is jeopardized?

More liberal branches of Judaism will take a woman's emotional health and well-being into account also. However, as far as a woman having the absolute right to abortion for any reason or no reason at all, it is not likely you will find an organized branch of Judaism to support this position.

— 84 —

THE IMPORTANCE OF NAMING CEREMONIES
AND THE CIRCUMCISION RITUAL

While there are no formalities governing how a child's name is determined in the Jewish culture, specific ceremonies do exist for naming children. These ceremonies differ depending on a child's gender. The covenant of circumcision (*berit milah*) occupies a principal place in Judaism, and male children must undergo the circumcision ceremony known as the *bris* (or *brit*, as it is pronounced in Israel).

Berit milah is probably the most observed commandment in Judaism. It is the first mitzvah from God that applies specifically to the Jewish people. In Genesis 17:10–12, God said to Abraham, "As for you, you and your offspring to come throughout the ages shall keep My covenant. . . . Every male among you shall be circumcised. You shall circumcise the flesh of your foreskin, and that shall be the sign of the covenant between Me and you. And throughout the generations, every male among you shall be circumcised at the age of eight days." This command has clear specifications, and the berit milah is performed on the eighth day after birth.

Since the covenant between God and the Jews was made with Abraham, and until that time Abraham's people did not practice circumcision, he was uncircumcised. However, it is written in the Torah (Genesis 17:24) that Abraham circumcised himself—at ninety-nine years of age.

The Jews were not the first people to practice circumcision. It was a custom among the ancient Egyptians, Ethiopians, Syrians, and Phoenicians, and appeared in parts of Africa, India, Australia, Indonesia, and the Philippines. Most Eskimos and Native Americans also circumcised their male children.

There may be health benefits to circumcision, and doctors commonly perform it as a medical procedure on newborn baby boys. However, this has nothing whatsoever to do with the practice in Judaism carried out to satisfy this mitzvah, which marks an outward sign of the covenant between God and the Jewish people.

Those Jews who choose to circumcise their child need to decide whether a *mohel* or a physician should perform the operation. The mohel is a specialist trained both in the medical and the religious aspects of the berit milah. However, the mohel is usually not a physician. In recent years, more circumcisions have been performed in the hospital than in the home by a mohel, or in the synagogue, as is the custom of Sephardic Jews. However, a medical circumcision does not fulfill the mitzvah.

Today, a doctor can carry out the medical procedure with a rabbi conducting the religious component, or it's possible to find a physician who has been trained in the religious aspects of circumcision. Another option is to arrange for a mohel to conduct the berit milah anew, after a physician has performed the circumcision. In such a case, the mohel will only take a symbolic drop of blood to satisfy the physical requirement (a ritual known as *hatafat dam berit*). At any rate, the mohel uses a double-edged knife to make certain the cut is swift and clean, so a baby does not endure unnecessary pain.

In terms of the actual ceremony, custom has it that Jewish parents do not invite friends and family to the bris. Instead, they inform everyone when the event is scheduled with the understanding that they may come if they wish.

As the ceremony begins, the parents bring the baby into the room and carefully place him on the special chair set aside for the prophet Elijah, who is said to watch over all circumcisions. The baby is then laid on the lap of the *sandek*, or godfather (often the child's grandfather), who is seated on another chair.

Several blessings and prayers are made before, during, and after the circumcision. Following the circumcision, a blessing is made over the wine and a drop is placed on the baby's lips. At this time the baby boy is given his formal Hebrew name.

As with all joyous events, a festive meal follows. The baby boy now has a name and has fulfilled the mitzvah to mark the covenant of the Jewish People with God.

But what about naming ceremonies for girls? Obviously, baby girls are not circumcised, and there is no female equivalent of the berit milah. While there are no explicit rituals or mitzvot associated with the birth of a baby girl, customs and traditions have evolved to celebrate this equally important occasion.

Traditionally, a baby girl receives her name either when her father is honored with an aliyah on the first Sabbath after she is born or during any Torah reading. A prayer is said at this time for the health and well-being of the mother and child. If the mother is present, she recites a special prayer of thanksgiving.

In Reform congregations, it is the common practice to name a baby girl during a Friday evening or Saturday morning service where the parents are in attendance with their friends and family.

However, a baby may be named in places other than the synagogue. Some parents prefer to name their baby girls in their home and invite family and friends to participate in a celebration. This ceremony is called a *berit ha-chayim* (the covenant of life) or *berit ha-bat* (the covenant for a daughter). During this ceremony, the baby girl is given her name.

In naming a baby girl, the prayer recited by Ashkenazic Jews begins with the patriarchs: Abraham, Isaac, and Jacob. When Sephardic Jews name a baby girl at a Torah reading, the blessing that is customarily made begins with the matriarchs: Sarah, Rebecca, Rachel, and Leah.

—— 85 ——

REDEMPTION CEREMONIES

In Judaism, one of the 613 commandments proclaimed by God is that every firstborn male among the Hebrews belongs to God and must be sanctified. The idea of "first" has always held a special position in Judaism. For instance, the Torah specifies that the first fruits and firstborn kosher animals had to be brought to the priests at the Temple. The first of all things belong to God, and this principle applies to children as well.

In some cultures during biblical times, this would have required nothing less than a physical sacrifice of the newborn baby. However, God decreed an additional mitzvah by providing for the redemption of the child.

Another explanation for this tradition has to do with the Exodus from Egypt, when God spared the firstborn Jewish males from the final plague (see number 3). Because the Jews are indebted to God for the firstborn males, they should be redeemed.

Redemption is not necessary if the firstborn is a girl, because the tenth plague never placed the lives of firstborn females in jeopardy. (In this case, any children thereafter are not subject to redemption.) Moreover, the mother of the firstborn male child must be Jewish. Otherwise, according to traditional Judaism that follows the matriarchal bloodline, the child is not Jewish and is not subject to this commandment. Family lineage also plays a role when it comes to this ritual. If either the father or mother is a kohein or Levite, redemption is not necessary.

Things get even more technical because the mitzvah specifically refers to the firstborn as one who "opens the womb." Therefore, a child delivered by cesarean section does not fall within the definition and is not redeemed. If subsequent children are born in the traditional fashion, most believe redemption does not apply in such instances. In cases of miscarriage or stillbirth, there is no redemption for any children born later. As for twin boys, the first one out of the gate gets redeemed!

The redemption ceremony is called *Pidyon Ha-Ben*, which literally means "redemption of the son." Some families have developed a parallel ceremony for firstborn girls, called *Pidyon Ha-Bat*. The ritual must take place on the thirty-first day of the child's life or as soon as possible thereafter. Since a monetary transaction is involved, the ceremony may not occur on Shabbat or on any biblical holiday. While it is traditional for Ashkenazic Jews to conduct the ceremony during the day, Sephardic Jews usually perform it at night.

Although not necessary, it is desirable to have a *minyan* (ten Jewish adults) during the ceremony, but the father of the child and a kohein must be present. Appropriate blessings are made for washing the hands and breaking the bread. At this time, the redemption is made and then the meal is eaten.

In preparation for the ceremony, the appropriate sum of money is set aside on an ornate tray (preferably silver). In the Torah, the amount to be paid was set at five *sela'im* (equal to about 100 grams of silver). Today, this sum translates to about $4 or $5, in silver dollars, if possible.

Traditionally, the baby is placed on another tray and the father carries his son to the kohein. As he holds the boy on the tray, the kohein performs a brief ritual, which includes blessings and recitations. During the ceremony, the father hands over the money to the kohein and the kohein blesses the child. A blessing is made over the wine and the gathered people enjoy a festive meal.

If the mother is Jewish but the father is not, the firstborn male should be redeemed by the mother. However, it is advisable for the boy to perform the redemption again after reaching the age of thirteen without reciting the customary blessings.

— 86 —

BAR AND BAT MITZVAH: BECOMING SONS AND DAUGHTERS OF THE COMMANDMENT

As Jewish children grow up, they are introduced to Judaism, the Hebrew language, Jewish celebrations and rituals, Jewish history and traditions, and, of course, the Torah. Bar mitzvah and bat mitzvah (and to a much lesser extent, confirmation—see number 89) mark the way of each Jewish child along the road to adulthood. This milestone marks the moment when a Jewish young person assumes his or her place in the Jewish community.

Bar mitzvah literally translates as "son of the commandment" (*bar* is Aramaic for "son"), and *bat mitzvah* (pronounced *bas mitzvah* by the

Ashkenazim) means "daughter of the commandment," since *bat* is Hebrew and Aramaic for "daughter."

According to Jewish law, children should be taught the ways of Judaism. They are encouraged to observe as many of the rituals and obligations as they can, but they are not required to comply with the mitzvot until they become adults—until the bar or bat mitzvah. Once they become adults in the eyes of Jewish law, the duty arises to abide by God's commandments.

Possibly the most pervasive misunderstanding Jews have about Judaism is the notion that in order to become a bar mitzvah or bat mitzvah, they must do so in a ceremony conducted in the synagogue. This error results from a misreading of what bar mitzvah and bat mitzvah mean.

In Judaism, there is no option of deciding whether or not to be bound to the commandments. It is a responsibility that comes with the covenant God made with Abraham and the Jews for all generations to follow. It is automatic. At the age of thirteen, a boy becomes a bar mitzvah. From then on, he is expected to keep the mitzvot Jewish men are required to fulfill. At the age of twelve, a girl becomes a bat mitzvah, which means that she is now obligated to carry out the mitzvot pertaining to Jewish women. (The reason girls assume this responsibility at a younger age probably has to do with the fact that girls mature faster than boys at this time of their lives.) Again, no ceremony is required in the case of either gender. Rituals and practices are not needed—the festive party that is common today is just an added bonus.

Becoming a bar mitzvah also confers certain rights under Jewish law.

(Some of these laws may also apply to girls who are bat mitzvah, depending upon the branch of Judaism involved.) These rights include the following:

- The right to participate in or lead a religious service
- The right to count toward a minyan
- The right to enter into binding contracts
- The right to provide testimony in religious courts

While the ages of twelve and thirteen for a girl and boy, respectively, mean they are adults insofar as fulfilling mitzvot, this does not suggest that young people are adults in every sense of the word. For example, according to Jewish law, marriage should take place no earlier than at sixteen years of age, and the suitable age to enter the work force is considered to be twenty.

Although a specific ceremony is not required for becoming a bar mitzvah or a bat mitzvah, a ceremony that celebrates this rite of passage does exist. It generally takes place after the boy or girl has completed several years of Hebrew and Judaic studies. Bar mitzvah and bat mitzvah ceremonies are beautiful events that mark an important occasion in a young person's life.

87

The bar and bat mitzvah ceremonies

The bar mitzvah ceremony is not mentioned in the Bible or the Talmud, and the practice probably has its origins in the Middle Ages. Because the ceremony does not actually denote when a young man becomes a bar mitzvah, it can occur anytime after his thirteenth birthday. If studies and preparation have not been completed, it is wise to postpone the ritual.

Because there are no mitzvot governing the ceremony, practices vary among the respective movements in Judaism and even from congregation to congregation. However, some common elements usually occur.

Probably the oldest and most universal aspect of the ritual is that it takes place during a Shabbat service soon after the boy's thirteenth birthday. During that morning, the young man is called to the Torah to recite a blessing and the weekly Torah reading.

In more recent years, the bar mitzvah generally chants the *Haftorah* (the concluding reading from the Prophetic section of the Bible). The bar mitzvah may read the entire Torah portion, conduct part of the service, lead the congregation in selected prayers, or make a speech.

Furthermore, the rabbi may speak to the bar mitzvah boy about the significance of the occasion, and the congregation may present the boy with gifts such as books or ritual items. When the service is concluded, a feast or party often follows.

Unless the bar mitzvah is an Ashkenazic Orthodox Jew, the bar mitzvah ceremony will mark the first time he wears a *tallit* (ceremonial prayer shawl). Ashkenazic Orthodox men do not wear the tallit until they get married.

The first bat mitzvah ceremony took place on Saturday morning, March 18, 1922. On that Shabbat, Judith Kaplan, the twelve-year-old daughter of Rabbi Mordecai Kaplan (the founder of Reconstruction-ism—see number 13), stepped up to the bimah of her father's synagogue, the Society for the Advancement of Judaism in New York. She recited the preliminary blessing and read from the Torah. This was a startling, bold, and innovative event designed to support Mordecai Kaplan's objective for Jewish women to have equal standing with Jewish men.

Over the next two decades, few women participated in the bat mitz-vah ceremonies, probably because the Reconstructionist movement did not grow substantially until the late 1960s. The Conservative movement actually became responsible for the growing popularity of the bat mitz-vah ceremony.

The Reform movement did not play an active role in this issue for the simple reason that it was questioning the necessity of even having this type of ceremony—whether bar or bat mitzvah—in the first place. In the Reform movement, some boys and girls underwent a confirmation cer-emony (as described later in number 89).

As of 1940, only a handful of Conservative congregations had adopted bat mitzvah rituals, but by the end of that decade, more than a third of the movement's member synagogues had established the ceremony. A mere twenty years later, this practice was the norm among Conservative congregations. However, during the formative years of this ceremony, the bat mitzvah did not read from the Torah and even today, some Conservative synagogues still refrain from this practice.

By the 1950s, only a third of Reform temples conducted a bat mitzvah ceremony, but a decade later it was widespread within the movement. Today, in Reform and Reconstructionist congregations alike, the bat mitzvah sings the blessings and reads from the Torah portion—the ceremony is essentially the same as a bar mitzvah.

Among the Orthodox, there is no similar type of bat mitzvah ceremony in the synagogue since women are not called to the Torah. However, many Orthodox do celebrate the occasion of a girl becoming a bat mitzvah with a festive party or some type of ceremony.

88

PARTIES, FEASTS, AND OTHER ACTIVITIES
TO CELEBRATE BAR AND BAT MITZVAHS

Following the religious bar or bat mitzvah ceremony, family and friends have a celebration called a *seudat mitzvah*—a feast that celebrates the fulfillment of a commandment. Although in this case the commandment was attained automatically when the young person reached the appropriate age (and not by way of the ceremony), a celebration is still in order.

The bar or bat mitzvah feast should be an opportunity to impress upon young men and women the responsibilities and obligations to fulfill the commandments that accompany reaching this milestone in their lives. The decorum ought to reflect the seriousness of the occasion. A meal is always appropriate, and there can be festive dancing and music. But this should also be a time for discussions about subjects of Jewish interest, particularly with the new son or daughter of the commandment in mind.

When it comes to bar and bat mitzvah extravaganzas, one-upmanship has become almost routine. This is true, albeit to varying extents, for all the branches of Judaism. Although bar and bat mitzvah galas were unheard of a hundred years ago, such spectacles have frequently become the focus in contemporary American society.

What messages do such displays convey to the new son or daughter of the commandment? Do such affairs add to or detract from the mitzvah they are meant to celebrate? Can something better or more appropriate be done? People are beginning to ponder such issues.

Clearly, there are many options and activities that can underscore and complement what it means to become a bar mitzvah or bat mitzvah. Lavish affairs do not do this. *Tzedakah* (charity) does. These days, more and more Jews are adhering to the concept of *tikkun olam* (repair of the world) and are making this part of the bar and bat mitzvah parties and feasts.

For example, why not deliver the party's leftover floral arrangements to a senior citizen home or a hospital? How about making sure all that extra food is sent to a homeless shelter? And speaking of the homeless and the poor, what about asking guests to bring canned food and used clothing that can be distributed to those in need? Why not arrange to have a tree planted in Israel in honor of every person who is called to light a candle on the bar or bat mitzvah cake? And what better way to stress the importance of mitzvot that require giving to those less fortunate than by setting aside a portion of the gifts received and donating them to charities the young man or woman selects?

Some people believe that rather than spending many thousands of dollars for an affair that's over in one night, the funds are better put to use to finance a family trip to Israel. After all, *Eretz Yisrael* (the Land of Israel) is a land steeped in the history of the Jewish People, where the events recounted in the Bible come alive and where people can see actual sites firsthand. Israel is a nation populated with Jews of every ilk—Sephardic and Ashkenazic, religious and secular, hailing from countries all over the world, all coming together in the Jewish homeland.

This has become such a popular idea that it's not difficult to find organized groups from an array of organizations, synagogues, and tours. Sometimes, either in addition to or in lieu of a bar or bat mitzvah ceremony in a young person's own synagogue, people even choose to hold the ceremony in Israel.

——— 89 ———

CONFIRMATION: CELEBRATING CONTINUED EDUCATION

Confirmation provides young men and women with a unique opportunity to continue their Jewish education after they become a bar or bat mitzvah. The confirmation ceremony is a recent addition to Judaism. Interestingly, it is an outgrowth of a negative reaction to bar mitzvah and bat mitzvah ceremonies held in a synagogue.

In the mid-nineteenth century, as Reform Judaism moved away from traditional customs and observances, the bar mitzvah ceremony came into question. For a period of time, Reform temples even stopped holding bar mitzvah ceremonies altogether. Instead, the Reform movement introduced group confirmation ceremonies that marked the completion of a course of Jewish education for Jews between the ages of fifteen and eighteen. (Since Reform congregations abandoned the bar mitzvah ceremony, it fell upon the Conservative movement to promote the idea of a bat mitzvah ceremony once Mordecai Kaplan introduced the ritual—see number 87.)

While the Reform movement eventually reinstated bar mitzvah ceremonies and added the bat mitzvah ceremonies as well, the concept of a group confirmation service had become entrenched. In fact, the Conservative and Reconstructionist movements, as well as some modern Orthodox congregations, also adopted confirmation, and it is a widespread practice today.

This rite-of-passage occasion commonly takes place at the age of sixteen, following three additional years of Jewish education after the bar or bat mitzvah event. Typically, congregations hold this group ceremony on Shavuot. Together as a class, the young men and women often perform a cantata or drama. The service may include a Torah reading, special music, speeches, a blessing from the rabbi, and floral arrangements.

Friends and family fill the sanctuary, taking pride not so much in the ceremony itself but in the fact that the confirmands spent several additional years learning about Judaism and the history and culture of the Jewish people. Of course, this does not mean that they have reached the end of their Jewish education—there is always more to learn. Throughout each Jewish person's adult life, there are numerous forums and opportunities to study Judaism and the myriad topics connected with the rich tradition of the Jewish people. Each Jew has not just the opportunity but also the responsibility to continue learning for the rest of his or her life.

— 90 —

JEWISH FUNERAL CEREMONIES

In any culture, one of the chief purposes of the funeral service is to pay reverence to the deceased. During the Jewish funeral service, a rabbi reads selected prayers and psalms, including *El Malei Rachamim*, a prayer that asks for repose of the departed soul. Carrying on a tradition that began with Abraham, who eulogized his wife Sarah (Genesis 23:2), a eulogy is given to praise the departed one and to express the grief felt by family and friends.

Before the chapel service or at the graveside service, the ritual of *Keriah* (tearing) is performed. This involves rending (tearing) one's garments as a display of separation. The practice has its origins in Genesis 37:34, where "Jacob rent his garments" when informed (erroneously) that his son, Joseph, was killed by a wild animal. The garments may also be torn immediately upon hearing of the death of a loved one. In lieu of tearing up their clothes, some Jews wear a black ribbon.

Some people tear their garments as an act of mourning for a parent, child, sibling, or spouse. Others tear their clothes in mourning for their parents but wear a black ribbon for all other relatives.

A wooden casket (frequently pine) is used in Jewish burials, perhaps because wood decomposes at about the same rate as the body. Therefore, the body can return more rapidly to dust. In Israel, caskets are not used; the body is buried wrapped in a prayer shawl.

It is Jewish custom that the family and friends physically assist in the burial, throwing clumps of earth over the coffin. Those gathered at the grave then say the *Kaddish*, a prayer in Aramaic that is commonly used in mourning rituals. Interestingly, this traditional prayer for the dead doesn't discuss death, it exalts God and appeals for world peace. The Kaddish marks the end of the burial service.

From that point on, when the deceased has been given due respect and the body properly buried, the person who passed away is no longer the focus of attention. The concern now must focus on the mourners, whose sense of anguish at the loss of a loved one does not cease as the last shovel of earth is thrown over the grave. In recognition of mourners' feelings, and in order to pay proper deference to the memory of the departed one, Judaism has specific procedures in place for the period of mourning, which will be explained in numbers 91 and 92.

— 91 —

WHAT DOES SITTING SHIVA MEAN?

As noted in number 90, beyond funeral and burial services, there are other practices that relate specifically to mourning. Jewish mourning customs serve two purposes: to demonstrate respect for the deceased and to provide solace for the mourners. There are four distinct stages of mourning. The first, *aninut*, encompasses the time period between death and interment (see number 29.) Next is *shiva*, which begins immediately after burial. (You'll learn about the final two phases of mourning, shloshim and avelut, in number 92.)

If you are not Jewish, you've probably heard the term "sitting shiva" used before, but you might not know exactly what that means. Shiva is a period that lasts for seven days (*shiva* is Hebrew for "seven"). The day of burial is included in the shiva period and counts as the first day. In some less traditional communities, shiva is observed for three days.

Parents, siblings, spouse, and children of the deceased sit shiva at the home of the deceased or at one of the mourners' homes. They go directly to the shiva house from the cemetery, wash their hands before entering (as does everyone who leaves a funeral), light a candle that will remain burning throughout the shiva period, and begin to sit shiva.

The meal of consolation, *seudat havra'a*, is the first meal served to mourners. Friends often provide it. Traditionally, this meal consists of hard-boiled eggs, bagels, and dairy products. The circular shape of some of these foods is intended to be symbolic of the eternal nature of life.

There are a number of observances and prohibitions that should be followed during shiva. The following is a list of some of these interdictions and observances. Mourners should:

- Cover all the mirrors in the house
- Avoid bathing, shaving, or cutting their hair or nails
- Refrain from wearing leather shoes
- Avoid washing their clothes or wearing new clothes (except clothes to be worn on Shabbat)
- Abstain from sexual relations
- Avoid conducting business
- Limit leaving the shiva house
- Sit on a low stool, bench, or on the floor

It is a mitzvah to comfort a mourner, so making a shiva call is encouraged. The first three days of shiva are generally reserved for visits from family and close friends. Those who did not know the deceased as well should hold off until the first three days have passed. However, if a person will not be able to visit later, it is better to visit during the first three days than not at all. Naturally, if shiva is observed for only three days, any time during that period is appropriate.

Because the mourners say their prayers and the *Kaddish* (prayer of mourning) at the shiva house, they must rely upon guests to make up the minyan. As for decorum, the basic guideline is just to be present, which, in and of itself, brings comfort to mourners. It is more important to listen than to speak, and it is even customary not to say hello or good-bye, since the mourner is forbidden to extend greetings and salutations. However, upon leaving, it is traditional to say to the mourner, "May God comfort you among the other mourners of Zion and Jerusalem."

Should Shabbat fall within the shiva period, it is counted as a day even though it is not observed as a day of mourning. If a major festival (Rosh Hashanah, Yom Kippur, Passover, Shavuot, or Sukkot) falls during shiva, then shiva comes to an abrupt end. When a death occurs on a major holiday, everything is delayed, including the burial, until the holiday is over.

Shiva ends on the afternoon of the seventh day following a burial. At that time, it is customary for the mourners to leave the shiva house and take a walk, accompanied by friends and family. This excursion indicates that the mourners are ready to return to the external world from which they had withdrawn. At this time, the remaining stages of mourning begin (see number 92).

—92—

THE FINAL PHASES OF MOURNING

After shiva, the third period of mourning in the Jewish tradition is called *shloshim*. This period extends to the thirtieth day after burial (*shloshim* is Hebrew for "thirty"). During shloshim, some prohibitions that apply to shiva remain in place, including the restriction on cutting nails or hair, wearing new clothes, shaving, attending parties, or listening to music.

The final period of mourning, which only applies to those who have lost a parent, is *avelut*, a mourning period of twelve months. Keep in mind that this final period of mourning lasts for twelve months and is based on the Hebrew calendar, which sometimes has a "leap" month, the second month of Adar. During a leap year, when a thirteenth month is added, avelut should be observed for only twelve months and not the entire year.

During the time of avelut, mourners abstain from parties, celebrations, and other entertainment. However, the mourners should otherwise make it a point to begin their return to a normal life. Other practices are observed in memory of the departed. Throughout the year of mourning, at the end of every prayer service each mourner should recite the Kaddish. Commonly known as the mourner's prayer, remember Kaddish is really a prayer of praise to God and has nothing to do with death or mourning. The importance of reciting the Kaddish is that it's performed standing up at public prayer. Through this public exaltation of God, the mourner demonstrates a reaffirmation of faith even after the death of a loved one.

At specific times of the year (Yom Kippur, Passover, Shavuot, and Sukkot), mourners also need to recite the *Yizkor* prayer. Yizkor (Hebrew for "may [God] remember") is the abridged popular name for the memorial service, *Ha-Zkarat Neshamot* (Remembrance of the Souls). At this service, congregants remember their loved ones who have passed on but also commemorate all those who died sanctifying God's name—for instance, the fighters of Israel's War of Independence. Some congregations make this an occasion to remember the six million Jews murdered by the Nazis. It is suitable to begin saying Yizkor either at the first holiday after the death of a loved one or at the first opportunity that takes place at the end of the twelve-month mourning period.

Another practice that continues to be observed past mourning is the lighting of a *Yahrzeit* candle. Yahrzeit occurs on the annual anniversary of the date of death, as set by the Hebrew calendar. At this time, in addition to reciting the Kaddish, a twenty-four-hour candle is lit in the home and, often, in the synagogue in memory of the departed person. This burning light of the Yahrzeit candle is symbolic of the immortal soul.

Jewish law requires a tombstone to mark the grave of the deceased so that the departed one will not be forgotten and the grave will not be desecrated. While the tombstone can be erected anytime after shloshim, in many communities it is customary either to refrain from setting up the tombstone or to keep it veiled until the end of the twelve-month mourning period.

Some time before the end of the year of mourning (usually around eleven months), the mourners hold a ceremony to dedicate the grave marker. This ceremony is generally referred to as an "unveiling" (*Ha-Kamat Matzeyvah*).

There are no specific requirements concerning how a tombstone must be inscribed. In some communities, it is customary to place small stones on the gravesite when visiting. The origin of this cultural practice is uncertain. A popular explanation states that in the desert environment of ancient Israel, mourners piled stones and rocks to prevent the sandy soil from blowing away and exposing the corpse.

Part 6

Jewish Custom, Culture, and Tradition

As you have seen throughout this book, Judaism is more than just a religion. Jews have been regarded as a "people," a "nation" (though one without a homeland for most of its existence), a "race," and a "culture." Indeed, Jews share more than their religion; they also have a common culture, though this might not always be easily apparent at first glance. Yet there is no one clear way of precisely defining what it means to be a Jew in the cultural sense, because Jews have traditionally called a number of disparate places their home, from Eastern Europe to the Middle East.

Given a history of almost 4,000 years and a geographic dispersal that forced the Jews to confront and often assimilate into a variety of cultures, Jewish culture has never been homogeneous. Nevertheless, in spite of this amalgam of nationalities, there are certain cultural elements—such as common language, themes in literature, and types of food—that have come to be recognized as quintessentially "Jewish." Somehow, all of the diverse customs and practices have managed to come together, much like Joseph's coat of many colors. And like the variegated hues of Joseph's coat, the result has been truly wondrous and remarkable.

93

THE HEBREW LANGUAGE AS A COMMON THREAD

Language is a body of words and systems that are common to a people, community, or nation. The Hebrew language, used for worship and religious study by Jews all over the world—in places as distant as Yemen, Greece, and Poland—helped the Jewish people to retain their sense of commonality. Moreover, Jewish communities in various countries developed their own dialects, such as Yiddish, to use in everyday life.

For thousands of years and without interruption, Hebrew has been the universal language of Judaism used for prayer and worship. Hebrew is one of the world's oldest languages, dating perhaps as far back as 4,000 B.C.E. The early Hebrews conversed in Hebrew, a Semitic idiom of the Canaanite group that includes Arabic. The patriarchs spoke Hebrew as they made their way into the Promised Land, and it remained the language of the Hebrews throughout the biblical period.

However, in the fifth century B.C.E., when Jews began to return to Israel from Babylon, where many had lived after the destruction of the First Temple in 586 B.C.E., most of the inhabitants of Palestine conversed in Aramaic, which gradually infiltrated the Hebrews' language. A few centuries later, Hebrew had all but ceased to exist as a spoken language. It would not be reestablished as such for two millennia.

Today, many observant Jews take on the task of studying Hebrew. Hebrew is not the easiest language to learn. For starters, it is read from right to left, just the opposite of reading English. Those who study Hebrew also have to learn a new alphabet with twenty-two consonants, five of which assume a different form when they appear at the end of a word. And if this isn't enough of a challenge, Hebrew is generally written without vowel sounds!

Actually, the absence of vowels is common in Semitic languages. The convention dates back to Hebrew's earliest days, when most people were fluent in the language and had no need for vowels in order to read it. However, literacy declined, especially after the destruction of the Second Temple when the Jews commenced their 2,000-year-long Diaspora. Sometime around the eighth century C.E., rabbis came up with an answer to help increase the number of Jews who could become literate in Hebrew—the *nikkudim* (points), a system of dots, dashes, and lines that are situated just about anywhere (above, below, beside, or inside the consonants). Most nikkudim indicate vowels; when nikkudim appear in the text, it is called pointed text and is obviously easier to read.

While nikkudim appear in prayer books and in many texts, especially books for children, only the consonants are used in Torah scrolls or the parchment inside *tefillin* (leather boxes that contain scrolls with scripture passages, bound to the arm and forehead during Jews' morning prayer) and *mezuzot* (scrolls of parchment affixed to the doorpost).

The entire style of writing Hebrew in the sacred scrolls is different. In contrast to the block print that is customarily seen in Hebrew books, sacred documents are written in a style that utilizes "crowns" on many of the letters. These crowns resemble crows' feet that emanate from the upper points. This type of writing is known as "STA'M" (an abbreviation for *Sifrei, Torah, Tefillin,* and *Mezuzot*).

The Hebrew Alphabet

mem sophit (final *mem*)	ם	*aleph*	א
nun	נ	*bet*	ב
nun sophit (final *nun*)	ן	*gimel*	ג
samech	ס	*dalet*	ד
ayin	ע	*heh*	ה
pei	פ	*vav*	ו
phe sophit (final *phe*)	ף	*zayin*	ז
tzadi	צ	*chet*	ח
tzadi sophit (final *tzadi*)	ץ	*tet*	ט
kuf	ק	*yud*	י
resh	ר	*kaf*	כ
shin	ש	*khaf sophit* (final *khaf*)	ך
tav	ת	*lamed*	ל
		mem	מ

A more modern cursive form of writing is frequently employed for handwriting. Yet another style, *Rashi script*, appears in certain texts to differentiate the body of the text from the commentary. This kind of text, named in honor of Rashi, the great commentator on the Torah and Talmud, is used for the exposition.

Further, the Hebrew numerical system uses letters as digits in the same way that Roman numerals are letters of the Latin alphabet. In Hebrew, though, each letter of the alphabet has a corresponding numerical value. The first ten letters have values of one through ten; the next nine have values of twenty through 100, counting by tens; and the remaining letters have values of 200, 300, and 400, respectively.

Unlike the Roman numerical system where the order of the letters is important, in the Hebrew system the sequence of the letters is irrelevant. The letters are simply added to determine the total value.

Since every Hebrew word can be calculated to represent a number, Jewish mysticism has been painstakingly engaged in discerning the hidden meanings in words' numerical value. For example, the numerical value of the Hebrew word *chai* (life) is eighteen. Hence, it is a common practice to make charitable contributions and give gifts, especially for weddings and bar or bat mitzvahs, in multiples of eighteen.

94

THE SACRED LANGUAGE AND THE MOTHER TONGUE

Traditionally through the ages, Jewish women were not taught Hebrew, and so they spoke Yiddish, a vernacular that is a mix of Middle High German, with a measure of Hebrew, and touches of Slavic tongues and Loez (a combination of Old French and Old Italian). Naturally, Jewish women spoke Yiddish to their children, who, in turn, spoke it to their own children. Thus, Yiddish became known as *mame loshen*, the "mother's language," as opposed to Hebrew, *loshen ha-kodesh*, or "the sacred language."

Yiddish has a long and colorful history. It is primarily a language of Ashkenazi Jews, though even segments of this group have often avoided, and at times even snubbed, the language. Nonetheless, Yiddish holds a prominent place in the hearts and minds of millions of Jews the world over.

Yiddish traces its roots to the beginning of the second millennium C.E., when Jewish emigrants from northern France began to settle along the Rhine. These emigrants, who conversed in a combination of Hebrew and Old French, also began to assimilate German dialects. The written language consisted completely of Hebrew characters.

At the beginning of the twelfth century, after the horrific pogroms of the First Crusade, Jews migrated to Austria, Bohemia, and northern Italy, taking their new language, Yiddish, with them. When Jews were invited to enter Poland as traders, Yiddish incorporated Polish, Czech, and Russian language characteristics.

Yiddish served the Jewish people well because it was an adaptable and assimilative language, absorbing some traits of the tongues spoken in the places Jews lived. Consequently, even English words and phrases made their way into Yiddish after the waves of immigration into the United States by European Jewry at the end of the nineteenth and early twentieth centuries.

Keep in mind that, just because *Yiddish* means "Jewish" in Yiddish, that doesn't mean that these words are synonymous. Jews do not speak "Jewish." *Jewish* is an adjective, while *Yiddish* is a noun that describes a particular Jewish language.

Although Yiddish was the chief vernacular of Ashkenazi Jews, not all Ashkenazi Jews spoke Yiddish. For one thing, it was the vernacular not of scholars but of the ordinary people. The language for prayer and study remained Hebrew, although Yiddish was often used in *yeshivas* (religious schools) to discuss the texts. The fact that Yiddish had to do with the daily tasks of living is reflected in the language itself, and this is one of the factors that makes Yiddish such a unique and alluring language—one that is peculiarly Jewish.

Yiddish is a social language, replete with nicknames, terms of endearment, and more than a good share of expletives. It has its proverbs and proverbial expressions, curses for just about every occasion, and idioms that reflect the fears and superstitions of the times. To learn and know Yiddish is to understand the Jews who created and spoke the language hundreds of years ago.

Yiddish is not the only language to have developed within Jewish communities in the Diaspora. Over the centuries, there have been and remain other languages, dialects, and vernaculars Jews have used to converse amongst themselves. Many Sephardic Jews from Arab countries still speak a mix of Hebrew and Arabic, and Sephardic Jews have their own international language known as *Ladino* or *Judezmo*. Ladino is written in either Hebrew or Roman characters and is based upon Hebrew and Spanish. It made its appearance as early as the Middle Ages and it is still spoken in Turkey, North Africa, Palestine (Israel), Brazil, and other parts of South America.

In the first decades of the twentieth century, Yiddish was the daily language of an estimated 11 million Jews all over the world. A short time later, this number was reduced by more than half; by the middle of the twentieth century, the language could have been placed on the endangered species list.

Even at its apex in the early twentieth century, Yiddish had its detractors. German Jews, who were very much integrated in the greater German society, were embarrassed at what they considered to be a bastardized version of the sublime German language. In the United States, Sephardic Jews who had lived there for many generations were chagrined at the foreign tongue their "greenhorn" compatriots used. Furthermore, Zionists rejected Yiddish in favor of Hebrew, which they wanted to revive as the vernacular of a new Jewish state.

The most important factor in the rapid decline of Yiddish was the *Shoah* (Nazi Holocaust), which destroyed entire communities of Yiddish-speaking Jews. When the survivors immigrated to Israel, they discovered that Yiddish was frowned upon as a language of the "ghetto" that reflected a subservient mentality.

However, in recent decades Yiddish has shown itself to be as stubborn and resilient as the Jewish people themselves when it comes to threats of destruction and extinction. In the United States, colleges and universities offer Yiddish courses, and special organizations and groups promote Yiddish both in the United States and in Israel, where there is now a greater acceptance for the language.

95

HEBREW'S RENAISSANCE IN THE
NINETEENTH AND TWENTIETH CENTURIES

Travel through modern Israel, and you will see the Hebrew letters that Diaspora Jews associate with prayer books filling the pages of newspapers and magazines, blaring messages on billboards, posted on cereal boxes, and plastered all over for-rent signs. Some visitors find this nothing short of miraculous.

For most of the second millennium, Hebrew was rarely spoken other than during religious observances or by scholars studying Torah and other sacred tomes. However, in the nineteenth century, Hebrew underwent a renaissance. Thanks in large part to Eliezer ben Yehudah, a Lithuanian Jewish scholar and leader who dedicated himself to the revival of

Hebrew and introduced thousands of modern terms to the ancient language, Hebrew regained its status as a vernacular language.

Reinforcing Hebrew's rescue from near extinction as a spoken tongue, the twentieth-century Zionist movement decided that Hebrew should become the language of the modern State of Israel once the Jewish homeland was established. As a result, Hebrew was recognized as the official language of Jewish Palestine in 1922.

Naturally, additional adjustments had to be made to Eliezer ben Yehudah's earlier efforts to bring Hebrew up to date. After all, the language had lain dormant for thousands of years. Much was new in the way of technology and devices, and the world was a different place. Consequently, the Hebrew of worship and religious scholarship is not exactly the same as modern Hebrew accepted as the new State of Israel's official language in 1948.

There is a difference between the Sephardic and Ashkenazi way of pronouncing several Hebrew vowels and one consonant. Because Israel has adopted Sephardic pronunciation for modern Hebrew, most Ashkenazim are adopting the Sephardic method of pronunciation.

Today, more than four and a half million people speak modern Hebrew. While Hebrew is the principal language for Israeli Jews, it is also a second language for many Israeli Arabs and recent immigrants. And, of course, Jews living outside of Israel may also be fluent in modern Hebrew.

— 96 —

THE HISTORY OF YIDDISH LITERATURE

Although it was born as a spoken language, Yiddish eventually made headway in literature produced mainly in Eastern Europe and later in the United States. For instance, you are probably familiar with the musical *Fiddler on the Roof*, but did you know that it was inspired by the collection of stories titled *Tevye's Daughters*, written in Yiddish by Sholom Aleichem?

Unfortunately, while a multitude of rich and immensely attractive Yiddish stories, novels, poems, and essays exist, unlike the stories from *Fiddler on the Roof*, most Yiddish literature has never been translated.

Yiddish literature can be divided into three periods: the period of preparation, the classical age, and the postclassical period. The first of these is the longest, spanning seven centuries. During this time, most Yiddish literature consisted of devotional works whose purpose was to make Judaism more intelligible to ordinary people. Perhaps the most noteworthy of these writings is the *Tz'enah ur'enah*, a liberal reworking of the stories from the Pentateuch (the five books of Moses), written by Jacob ben Isaac Ashkenazi.

However, there were also other modes of expressing Yiddish literature during this period. Beginning in the twelfth century, roving Jewish minstrels wandered through Germany reciting Gentile romances in Yiddish. By the fifteenth century, books of poetry, stories, and folktales appeared in Yiddish. In 1686, the first Yiddish newspaper was published in Amsterdam.

In the eighteenth century, Yiddish was the language used by the Hasidim in recounting the numerous tales and stories of the Ba'al Shem Tov and the ensuing masters of the movement. But it would take another hundred years for Yiddish literature to truly come into its own.

The classical age of Yiddish literature was brief in duration but brilliant, bold, and beautiful in its bloom. This period commenced in the late nineteenth century and ended fifty years later. While there were many distinguished writers of Yiddish literature during this time, three stood at the forefront: Sholom Jacob Abramowitz, best known as Mendele Mokher Sefarim (Mendele the Itinerant Bookseller); Sholom Rabinowitz, known as Sholom Aleichem; and Isaac Leib Peretz. These three luminaries of Yiddish fiction wrote about everyday life in the *shtetl* (small Jewish villages in Eastern Europe) and in the pale of settlement in Russia.

Each made a unique contribution to the body of Yiddish literature. Mendele Mokher Sefarim was the first to employ Yiddish as a vehicle for literary creation. Sholom Aleichem was perhaps unequaled in his ability to depict the authentic human condition of his day with humor, gentleness, and profound sadness. Peretz, trained as a lawyer and the most intellectual and sophisticated of the three, provided a thread of psychological finesse in his work.

— 97 —

THE RISE OF MODERN JEWISH WRITING

In the early part of the twentieth century, as a result of wars, revolutions, and persecutions, many Yiddish writers fled Eastern Europe for the United States. Consequently, New York became a Yiddish literary center almost equal to Warsaw in stature. Notable during this time were Abraham Reisen, who wrote poetry and short stories, and Sholem Asch, who, along with Israel Joshua Singer, helped perfect the Yiddish novel. Israel Singer's younger brother, Isaac Bashevis Singer, emerged as one of the most well-known Yiddish writers of short stories and novels.

In the Soviet Union, Yiddish writers pursued themes of social realism. Among these writers, many of whom were murdered in the purge of Yiddish writers and poets during the Stalin era, were the poet Moshe Kulbak, the novelist David Bergelson, and short-story writer Isaak Babel.

Today, Yiddish is in decline, and despite renewed interest in Yiddish literature, little new work is forthcoming. However, Jewish literature that isn't written in Yiddish, both religious and secular, abounds. So much so, in fact, it could easily fill voluminous anthologies.

Wherever Jews live in respectable numbers, there is a presence of Jewish literature that augments their sense of oneness as a people. In the last fifty years, American Jewish literature has flourished—if, that is, you count all types of work written by Jewish writers as Jewish literature.

A variety of well-established Jewish American writers have achieved critical acclaim, including Saul Bellow, Henry Roth, Bernard Malamud, Philip Roth, Joseph Heller, Elie Wiesel, Chaim Potok, Cynthia Ozick, and Leon Uris. With young writers of fiction such as Michael Chabon, Myla Goldberg, Thane Rosenbaum, and Allegra Goodman, the future of Jewish literature in twenty-first century America is secure.

Not only have Israeli novelists had a great impact on Israelis, their work has been translated from Hebrew, making them accessible to Jewish communities around the globe. We have been fortunate to witness the likes of Aharon Appelfeld, S. Y. Agnon, A. B. Yehoshua, and Amos Oz, as well as the emergence of a new generation of gifted Israeli writers such as David Grossman and Etgar Keret.

——— 98 ———

YIDDISH POETRY, DRAMA, JOURNALISM, AND MUSIC IN THE TWENTIETH CENTURY AND BEYOND

Yiddish poetry gained literary merit in the twentieth century. Many Yiddish poets emigrated to the United States and Israel, where their new milieu helped shape their work. For example, Morris Rosenfeld, who lived on the Lower East Side of Manhattan, wrote poetry protesting the inhumane conditions of the slums and sweatshops. Other notable poets were Simon Samuel Frug, Hayyim Nahman Bialik, and Chaim Grade, whose poetry frequently dealt with the Holocaust.

Yiddish drama began to take hold with the establishment of theaters in Romania, Odessa, Warsaw, and Vilna toward the end of the nineteenth century. However, the Russian government closed numerous Yiddish theaters in the 1930s, sending actors scurrying for safer shores. With many of these thespians settling in the United States, New York soon became the hub for Yiddish theater.

Yiddish newspapers not only provided a way for Yiddish writers to make a living but also offered an outlet for their fiction. A number of Yiddish tabloids published stories and columns for readers who couldn't always afford books. In 1863, the weekly *Kol Mevasser* was founded in Odessa, and in 1865, the first Yiddish daily newspaper, *Yiddishes Tageblat*, began publication in New York City. Perhaps the most renowned of the Yiddish papers was *The Jewish Forward*, a Yiddish daily founded in 1897. It is still in publication today, although it is now a weekly, published in English with a special Yiddish edition.

Along with a recent resurgence of the Yiddish language, Yiddish literature has become more accessible, particularly with the publication of anthologies. How long this revival will last remains to be seen. Yiddish, unlike Hebrew, is not the holy tongue of Judaism, and is not shared by all Jews. As the demographics of Jewish communities change, there is less incentive for Jews to learn Yiddish, and with each generation less and less people know how to speak it.

Like Jewish literature, Jewish music has played a large part in binding the Jewish people together, particularly during the Diaspora. Jewish music is a mammoth topic that can never be fully summarized in a book such as this one. Suffice it to say, today there is a resurgence of Jewish music called *klezmer music*, reminiscent of the times when groups of itinerant musicians went from village to village in Eastern Europe, entertaining the local Jewish populace with folk songs and folk dance as well as traditional music. Another branch of Jewish music is comprised of traditional and contemporary songs in Hebrew that originate from Israel.

— 99 —

JEWISH CUISINE

More than any other aspect of Jewish culture, Jewish food has held the Jews together all these years. Food plays an important part in many cultures, and the Jews are no exception. For the Jewish culture, food frequently serves both ethnic and religious functions. If you've read any number of other points in this book, by now you've surely noticed all Jewish holidays and festivals, no matter how major or minor, have at least one thing in common—there is always a feast (*seudah*). Technically, there probably is no such thing as "Jewish" food. There is, however, food that is not Jewish because it is not kosher and no amount of preparation will change that.

Obviously, food that complies with the laws of kashrut or is prepared accordingly is Jewish food. That's pretty much a no-brainer. Just as clearly, kashrut has helped keep the Jews together during the Diaspora. For example, if a Jew found himself in a strange town and he wanted to eat, he sought out a Jewish family or Jewish restaurant where he could have his meals. Even today, you will find sites on the Internet informing people about where they can have a kosher meal in various towns and cities.

Beyond the kosher element, Jewish food as a concept is really an amalgamation of many cultures. Many foods that can be considered "Jewish" are not exclusive to Jewish cuisine. Jewish food reflects the numerous places the Jews have lived over the centuries, including the influences of Middle Eastern, Spanish, German, Mediterranean, and Eastern European cooking styles. For example, hummus and falafel are common in much of the Middle East, stuffed cabbage is prevalent in Eastern Europe, and knishes are familiar to Germans as well as Jews.

Nevertheless, Jewish cuisine has developed a distinctive flair often applied to the foods and cooking techniques extracted from the lands in which Jews resided. A knack for economical cooking played its part here as well. In places where Jews were poor, particularly in the *shtetls* (small villages) of Eastern Europe, people had to make a few inexpensive ingredients go a long way, and this affected the manner of cooking.

As discussed in number 9, Sephardic and Ashkenazic Jews differ culturally (and sometimes even in minor matters of religion) as a result of having lived for centuries in different areas of the world. Just as they have their own respective dialects, ways of speaking Hebrew, particular religious practices, and cultural customs, they also have different ideas about Jewish cuisine. Subject to Mediterranean influences, Sephardic Jewish cuisine is characterized by the use of spices, olive oil, rice, and lamb, whereas Ashkenazi Jewish cooking reflects the Central, Northern, and Eastern European countries in which Ashkenazim lived.

For the most part, the food that Jews living in the United States generally consider "Jewish" corresponds more with Ashkenazi-style cooking. Some differences have been influenced by a slight American touch, while a few others have been created entirely in the Jewish-American tradition. In other words, it's a real mix, as you'll learn in number 100.

— 100 —

COMMON FOOD DISHES

As mentioned in number 99, much of the food Jews in America identify as "Jewish" stems from Ashkenazi cooking traditions, and this generally holds true regarding the fare mentioned in this point. Certain Jewish foods are associated with particular holidays because they are generally served on specific occasions. Of course, there is nothing wrong with serving these dishes throughout the year, which many Jewish families choose to do.

In the Jewish tradition, food dishes made with *matzah* (a flat bread made from a simple mix of flour and water without any eggs) abound. While matzah doesn't really have a flavor and is rather bland, some people do enjoy matzah all year round, eating it instead of crackers or bread. One good example is matzah ball soup, made of chicken broth and vegetables, like celery and carrots, with matzah balls floating in it. These matzah balls are known as *knaydelach* (Yiddish for "dumplings").

Some people also like matzah soaked in water and egg and then fried. There is even a Passover variation of *latkes* (potato pancakes, which are served on Hanukkah) that are made out of matzah meal.

As discussed at the beginning of Part 4, cooking is forbidden on Shabbat. To solve the problem of having to eat cold food, the Jews of Eastern Europe invented *cholent*, a slowly cooked stew of beans, barley, potatoes, and beef that can be started before Shabbat begins and then left to simmer. Another stew, a sweet one called *tzimmes*, consists of carrots, sweet potatoes, and/or prunes. Tzimmes is traditionally served on Rosh Hashanah and Passover.

The quintessential Jewish food item just might be the *bagel*. The word *bagel* is derived from the German *beugel*, which means "a round loaf of bread." Bagels are often topped with sesame seeds, poppy seeds, or touches of other flavors. However, the addition of cream cheese and lox is a custom born in America.

The *blintz* is another popular Jewish food item. The word *blintz* is really what might be called "Yinglish," because after Yiddish made its way to the United States, some English was incorporated into the language. The Yiddish word is actually *blintzeh* (from the Ukrainian for "pancake"), but blintzes bear a closer resemblance to crêpes than pancakes. A blintz is a flat pancake rolled around sweetened cottage cheese, mashed potatoes, jam, or fresh fruit and is frequently accompanied with sour cream or applesauce.

Other common Jewish food items include the following:

- **Borscht:** *Borscht* is beet soup, served either hot or cold. Eastern European Jews borrowed the borscht recipe from their Gentile neighbors. This dish became especially popular with the poor, who could afford readily available beets. When eating borscht, people often add sour cream.

- **Knishes:** A *knish* is a potato and flour dumpling normally stuffed with mashed potato and onion, chopped liver, or cheese. In fact, the word *knish* is Ukrainian for "dumpling."

- **Kreplach:** Another type of dumpling, triangular- or square-shaped *kreplach* (from the German *kreppel*) are similar to ravioli, contain cheese or meat, and are usually served in soup.

- **Kasha:** *Kasha* or *kasha varnishkes* is a mixture of buckwheat and bow-tie noodles. The term *kasha* comes from the Russian word for "porridge."

- **Kugel:** The term *kugel* comes from the German word for "pudding." The name is derived from the pan in which the pudding was baked and where it remained to be enjoyed throughout the Sabbath day. Kugel is either served as a casserole of potatoes, eggs, and onions, or as a desert made with noodles, fruits, and nuts in an egg-based pudding.

- **Stuffed cabbage:** *Stuffed cabbage* (also known as *holishke*, *praakes*, or *galuptzi*) can be prepared in a number of ways, including filling the cabbage with beef and then serving it in a sweet-and-sour sauce.

- **Kishkas:** The word *kishka* is derived from Russian and means "intestines" or "entrails." Originally, kishka was just that—entrails stuffed with meat, flour, and spices. Today, the intestines have been replaced with parchment paper or plastic.

- **Gefilte fish:** The word *gefilte* comes from German and it means "stuffed." Originally, gefilte fish was stuffed fish, but today it looks more like fish cakes or fish loaf. Gefilte fish may be made from a variety of fish, though it's most often made of carp. The fish is chopped or ground, then mixed with eggs, salt, onions, and pepper, or a vegetable mix. Traditionally, gefilte fish is served with horseradish.

There are many other Jewish dishes from which to choose, and the previous list has barely scratched the surface.

A few typical Jewish dishes, like chicken soup, are known for their medicinal value. At the other extreme, however, there is *schmaltz* (chicken fat, fried with onion and garlic), which has surely clogged many arteries. Not far behind schmaltz on the list of foods guaranteed to raise cholesterol and fat levels are corned beef, pastrami, tongue, and chopped liver— all of which have been part of the American Jewish diet.

But times are changing, and people have become more health-conscious in their dietary habits. What's more, there is also an increasing awareness of moral issues when it comes to eating animal products. Consequently, a number of Jewish vegetarian cookbooks contain traditional Jewish recipes without meat, fish, or fowl. Which just goes to prove that what is and what is not "Jewish food" has always been relative, and it probably always will be subject to change.

101

JEWISH HUMOR AS A MEANS OF SPEAKING ABOUT EXISTENTIAL QUESTIONS

According to the Bible, when God told Abraham that he and Sarah would have a son in their old age, Sarah's first reaction was to laugh in disbelief. Perhaps it was not a coincidence that the name they bestowed upon their son, Isaac (Yitzchak in Hebrew), who would become one of the patriarchs, means "laughter." (The Hebrew word for laughter is *tzechak*.)

Even as Abraham and Sarah, the first Jews, retained their sense of humor, throughout history, the Jews have never lost their particular sense of humor, despite all the hardships of exile and the persecution they have endured. Laughing at themselves often helped the Jews to survive and flourish. Humor does not become "Jewish" because it is about Jews. Nor, for that matter, are jokes considered "Jewish" because they were told or created by someone who happens to be Jewish. And yet it is not hard to tell when a joke or funny story fits into this category. Jewish humor has different themes, but it always speaks to the existential condition of the Jewish people.

To a large extent, Jewish humor is the result of the 2,000-year

Diaspora when the Jews lived without a "home" of their own. This perpetual exile was a source of both physical and emotional insecurity. While it is true there were shining moments in history, such as the Golden Age in Spain, they often ended with a period of Jewish persecution. In Spain, the Golden Age came to an end in 1492, when the Jews were told to convert to Christianity or else promptly depart.

In the face of such misfortunes and calamities, Jewish humor evolved into an affirmation of life. Gaiety and laughter were necessary to offset harsh and despairing conditions. In a way, the laughter generated by their humor was therapeutic—it assuaged the pain of persecution, grief, and poverty.

Jewish humor is more than a confirmation of life, however. It is a defiant answer to the question of why and how to go on, in spite of the terrible things that can occur in life. How else, when confronted by a hostile world for thousands of years, could this small band of people so audaciously cling to their beliefs and to Torah?

Jewish humor is often incisive and succinct. A number of motifs are woven through it. Whatever the forms or themes, Jews have a way of poking fun at themselves, as if saying to the world, "Hey, you can't malign us, we'll do it to ourselves!"

Jewish jokes also deal with the world in which the Jews live. And if the things they see aren't to their liking, criticism is freely dispersed. Some Jewish humorists, like Lenny Bruce, became critics of the societies in which they lived. At other times, Jewish humor conveyed a message and even encouraged certain types of moral conduct. Humor also had a way of deflecting the trauma endured by anti-Semitism.

Jewish humor is so vast it deserves a book by itself. In fact, there are many such books available, and Web sites with Jewish humor abound. Jewish humor reflects myriad themes. Some Jewish jokes focus on poverty, justice, and iconoclasm. These sorts of jokes remind Jews of the suffering of those who are less fortunate and of the mitzvah to give to the poor. Other jokes even exemplify the audacity of the Jews, who have never refrained from questioning God. Can it be any wonder, then, that throughout the centuries, this race of iconoclasts has never winced from challenging all forms of authority when justice was at stake?

Seeing the glass as half full and looking on the bright side of things are other themes frequently found in Jewish humor. And, indeed, an optimistic disposition has always been important in surviving the trials and tribulations Jews faced.

Historically, Jews have frequently faced discrimination that sometimes made access to higher education and other opportunities difficult. In such cases, the general response was to work twice as hard. No wonder jokes about how to succeed in the world also abound in Jewish culture. Sitting back, complaining, and merely hoping things would get easier is not how the Jews have made their way up the ranks of the societies in which they have lived. These sorts of jokes reflect the Jewish belief that everyone must work for whatever success they would like to achieve.

Jews also include humor that confronts the issues of anti-Semitism and survival in their repertoire of jokes. Such jokes demonstrate how utterly absurd anti-Semitism is, and how difficult it can be to convince those who harbor such ill will that their feelings are ludicrous. These types of jokes also demonstrate how Jews survived by their wits in societies where they had little else with which to defend themselves.

And the Jews did indeed survive. Over a span of four millennia, in hostile environs and under harsh conditions, subject to persecution and oppression, strengthened by their culture, shared history, and ethnic practices, the Jewish people have endured. They have also persisted because of shared beliefs, which, despite disparities and divergent opinions over the centuries, can nonetheless properly be called what we have come to know as Judaism.

Appendix

Timeline of Key Events:
Hinduism, Judaism, Christianity, Buddhism, and Islam

c. 1500–1200 B.C.: Rig-Veda Hymns written

c. 1300–1200 B.C.: Vedantism

c. 1230–1240 B.C.: Moses leads the Israelites out of bondage

1077–1037 B.C.: King David rules Israel

1027–997 B.C.: King Solomon rules Israel

c. 925: Israel splits into two states: Israel and Judah

858 B.C.: Elijah becomes a prophet of God

c. 850–750 B.C.: Brahmanism

739 B.C.: Isaiah is a prophet of God

722 B.C.: Israel falls to Assyria

c. 720 B.C.: Brahmanas written

c. 700 B.C.: Time of Shramanas (religious wanderers)

c. 600 B.C.: Aranyakas written

596 B.C.: Judah falls to Babylon

528 B.C.: Judeans return from Babylonian captivity

c. 560–480 B.C.: The life of Buddha (Siddhartha Gautama)

c. 509 B.C.: Israel and Judah fall under control of the Roman Empire

c. 500 B.C.: Hinduism

c. 479 B.C.: First council results in four Buddhist factions

c. 469 B.C.: Approximately sixteen Buddhist factions exist

c. 390 B.C.: Second Council declares Buddhist minority orthodox (Hinayana) and majority heretic (Mahayana)

c. 300 B.C.: Tantras written down

c. 300 B.C.: Buddhism arrives in Sri Lanka

300 B.C.–A.D. 30: Era of Sadducees, Essenes, Samaritans, Zealots, and Pharisees (precursors to Rabbinic Judaism)

297 B.C.: King Asoka converts to Buddhism; Buddhism grows from a small group to a major world religion, as Asoka sends out missionaries

247 B.C.: Asoka calls Third Council to agree on authentic Buddhist scriptures

200 B.C.–A.D. 200: Development of Hinayana Buddhism:

c. 50 B.C.: Buddhism arrives in China: Mahayana tradition develops

37 B.C.: Herod captures Jerusalem

4 B.C.–A.D. 30: Life of Jesus (begins his ministry A.D. 27)

A.D. 30: Pentecost: The birth of the Christian Church

30–600: The early Christian Church

35: Conversion of Saul, who becomes St. Paul

35–312: Age of Martyrs

42: Antioch is the center of Christian activity

c. 50: Vaishnavism

c. 64: Peter and Paul martyred in Rome

69: Bishop Ignatius consecrated in Antioch (St. Peter was the first bishop there; other early bishops of Antioch include James, Polycarp, and Clement)

c. 70: Saivism

70: Destruction of the Temple of Jerusalem

66–73: First Jewish War against Rome

c. 70–110: New Testament Gospels are written

99: Death of St. Clement, first Bishop of Rome and successor to St. Peter

c. 100: Composition of Bhagavad-Gita

100–200: As many as 500 Buddhist sects exist

150: St. Justin Martyr describes liturgical worship of the Church, centered in the Eucharist

132–135: Second Jewish War

c. 200: Laws of Manu compiled

200–300: Development of Mahayana Buddhism

300: Buddhism arrives in Japan

313: Constantine, emperor or Rome, embraces Christianity; Edict of Milan stops persecution of Christians (Constantine is not baptized until shortly before his death many years later)

320–600: Vajrayana Buddhism develops

325: The Nicene Creed is created at the Council of Bishops at Nicaea (the first of seven Ecumenical Councils)

330: Foundation of Constantinople

354–430: Life of St. Augustine of Hippo

381: First Council of Constantinople; Emperor Theodosius declares Christianity official religion of Roman Empire

387–493: Life of St. Patrick

397: Bishops at Carthage formalize New Testament

400: Completion of Jerusalem Talmud

400–600: Rise of Pure Land sects in China

410: Fall of Rome

451: Council of Chalcedon affirms apostolic doctrine of dual nature of Christ

c. 480–547: Life of St. Benedict, founder of Benedictine order

480: Bodhidharma goes to China as a Buddhist missionary

c. 500: Hindu Tantric tradition established

530: Founding of Benedictine order; the Benedictine Rule of monastic life served as the first constitution for monastic life and gave rise to other, subsequent Catholic monastic orders

538–597: Zhi-yi's life (founder of Tiantai)

c. 550: Tiantai school of Buddhism develops

553: Second Council of Constantinople

570–632: Life of Muhammad

447: A synod in Toledo, Spain, adds the *filoque* to the Nicene Creed, which asserts that the Holy Spirit proceeds from the Father and the Son

590–604: Pope Gregory I

c. 600: Beginning of Bhakti movement

c. 600–700: Shiah and Sufi branches of Islam develop

600–1300: Papal rule

638: Muslim conquest of Jerusalem

c. 640: Buddhism spreads to Tibet

c. 650: Tantrayana tradition, a radical reinterpretation of Mahayana Buddhism, develops

c. 650–750: Nara schools of Buddhism develop in Japan

691: Dome of the Rock built in Jerusalem

c. 700: Tendai school of Buddhism develops in Japan

711: Muslims begin to conquer Spain

732: Charles Martel halts Arab advance near Poitiers

749: First Buddhist monastery established in Tibet

c. 750: Development of Sephardic Judaism

787: Second Council of Nicaea, ending the era of Ecumenical Councils—restores the use of icons to the Church

800–1806: Holy Roman Empire

880: Photian Schism between Rome and Constantinople

c. 900–1300: Second revival of Buddhism in Tibet

c. 950–1000: Conversion of Europe to Christianity is completed

988: Conversion of Russia

c. 1000: Sunni branch of Islam develops

c. 1000s: Reform of Tantric tradition

c. 1000–1200: India encounters Islam; iconoclasm:

1054: Great Schism: Roman Catholic and Eastern Orthodox Churches split

1071: Battle of Manzikert

1073: Pope Gregory VII centralizes control of Church with new theory of papal superiority

1095–1254: The Crusades

c. 1150: Ashkenazic Judaism develops

c. 1150: Zen Buddhism develops in Japan

c. 1200s: Pure Land, Nichiren, and Zen sects develop in Japan

c. 1200s: Decline of Buddhism in Northern India

1204: Sack of Constantinople

1212: St. Francis creates the first of the mendicant orders, the Franciscans. The Dominicans, Carmelites, and Augustinians also arise in the 1200s

1224–1274: Life of St. Thomas Aquinas

1231–1834: The Inquisitions

c. 1250: Nichiren Buddhism develops in Japan

1291: Muslims seize Acre

1333: St. Gregory Palamas defends Orthodox practice of Hesychast spirituality (a form of Eastern monasticism) and the use of the Jesus prayer

1350–1700: European Renaissance

1377–1407: Great Papal Schism (struggle between Rome and Avignon)

1391–1475: Life of Dge-'Dun-Grub, first Dalai Lama

c. 1400s: Decline of Buddhism in Southern India

1469–c. 1539: Life of Nanak, Indian religious leader who broke from orthodox Hinduism and founded Sikhism

1453: Muslims seize Constantinople; end of Byzantine Empire

1483–1546: Life of Martin Luther

1492: Fall of Grenada

c. 1500s: Muslim influence on Hinduism

1509–1564: John Calvin's life

1517: Martin Luther nails his 96 Theses to the door of the Roman Church in Wittenberg

1517–1648: Protestant Reformation

c. 1523: Lutheran Church develops *

c. 1525: Anabaptists (leads to Mennonite and Amish)

1529: Church of England begins separation from Rome

c. 1534: Episcopalian: Henry VIII's Act of Supremacy

c. 1536: Calvinism

1540: Formation of the Jesuits

1542–1648: Catholic Counter-Reformation

1544: Jesuit missionary work begins in Japan, Africa, and North America

1545–1563: Roman Catholic Council of Trent

1559: John Calvin sends missionaries throughout Europe to convert Catholics to the new faith of Protestantism

c. 1560: Presbyterian

c. 1564: Puritan

1566: Pope Pius V standardizes Latin Mass

c. 1600: Sikhism

c. 1609: Baptist

1627–1682: Reign of Ngag-Dbang-Blo-Bzang Rgya-Mtsho, "Great Fifth" Dalai Lama

c. 1647: Quaker

1697–1790: The Enlightenment

1700–1760: Life of Yisra'El Ben Eli'ezer

c. 1700: Hasidic Judaism develops

c. 1700: Khalsa

1709–1791: Life of John Wesley

c.1738: Methodist

1760–1914: The Industrial Revolution

1782: First publication of *Philokalia*, a classic of spirituality

c. 1784: Shakers

1789: Protestant Episcopalian (U.S.)

1789: First Roman Catholic bishop (John Carrol) in the United States, and first diocese (the See of Baltimore)

1794: Introduction of Orthodoxy to North America when missionaries arrive on Kodiak Island in Alaska

c. 1830: *Book of Mormon* by Joseph Smith

1832: Church of Christ

1845–1848: Sikh Wars

c. 1849: Adventist

1854: Roman Catholic Dogma of Immaculate Conception

1869–70: First Vatican Council; Roman Catholic dogma of Papal Infallibility

1870: Jehovah's Witnesses

1869–1872: St. Nicholas establishes Japanese Mission

1863: Baha'i

1863: Seventh Day Adventist

1869–1948: Life of Mohandas Ghandi

1892: Church of Christ Scientist

1897: Zionist movement

1901: Pentecostal

1920s: Soviet Communism attack on Buddhism in Mongolia

1930: Nation of Islam (U.S.)

1933–1945: The Holocaust

1932: Saudi Arabia established

1945: Nag Hammadi Library discovered in Egypt

1948: State of Israel established

1950: Chinese communism attack on Buddhism

1952: World Fellowship of Buddhists formed

1962–1965: Second Vatican Council

1988: 1,000-year anniversary of Orthodoxy in Russia

1989: First woman ordained in Episcopal church

2000: Roman Catholic Jubilee

* **Note:** The branches of Protestantism mentioned in the timeline are by no means intended to be a comprehensive representation of all Protestant denominations. (At present, more than 500 Protestant denominations exist in the United States alone.) These denominations are meant to paint a fairly broad picture of some primary Protestant groupings, from which many other denominations stem. For more detailed information, refer to *www.laymanswalk.org/magazine/2002/2002.shtml*.

Sources: *The World Almanac*, 1998; *Encyclopedia Britannica, 15th Edition*, 1993; *The World's Religions*, Smart, 1998; *Illustrated Guide to World Religions*, Coogan, 1998; *World Religions from Ancient History to Present*, Parrinder, 1985; Conciliar Press, 1998; *Catholic Bible Apologetics, 1985–1997*.